Designing Next Generation Web Projects with CSS3

A practical guide to the usage of CSS3 – a journey through properties, tools, and techniques to better understand CSS3

Sandro Paganotti

PUBLISHING

BIRMINGHAM - MUMBAI

Designing Next Generation Web Projects with CSS3

First published: January 2013

Production Reference: 1140113

Published by Packt Publishing Ltd.
Livery Place
35 Livery Street
Birmingham B3 2PB, UK.

ISBN 978-1-84969-326-4

www.packtpub.com

Cover Image by Rakesh Shejwal (shejwal.rakesh@gmail.com)

Credits

Author
Sandro Paganotti

Reviewers
Berg Brandt
Angelos Evangelou
Andrew Wasson

Acquisition Editor
Usha Iyer

Lead Technical Editor
Ankita Shashi

Technical Editors
Manmeet Singh Vasir
Dominic Pereira

Copy Editors
Brandt D'Mello
Insiya Morbiwala
Aditya Nair
Laxmi Subramanian
Ruta Waghmare

Project Coordinator
Joel Goveya

Proofreaders
Denise Dresner
Kevin McGowan

Indexer
Monica Ajmera Mehta

Graphics
Aditi Gajjar

Production Coordinator
Nilesh R. Mohite

Cover Work
Nilesh R. Mohite

About the Author

Sandro Paganotti is a web developer, a Google Developers Expert in HTML5, a technical writer, and an HTML5/CSS3 teacher with a passion for Ruby and cutting-edge frontend technologies. He enjoys finding clever and pragmatic solutions to ambitious projects at Comparto Web, the company he co-founded in 2012.

He's also a funding member of WEBdeBs, a local community of web enthusiasts, and a speaker at local and national conferences.

I would like to thank everyone who developed the amazing libraries presented in this book, Lea Verou (also for this hint, "the first thing you can say about CSS3 is that it doesn't actually exist"), the teams behind Sass and Compass, Faruk Ateş, Paul Irish, and everyone who contributes to Modernizr, Richard Herrera for Flexie and Jason Johnston for CSS3 PIE. Also thanks to Sara Baroni and Paolo Dusi for their amazing infographic that I used in *Chapter 4, Zooming User Interface*.

A big thanks to Davide, Fabio, and Mattia, my partners at Comparto Web.

Another big thanks to my editors at Packt Publishing for their time, patience, and wise advice and to Alessandro Cinelli "cirpo" for his useful review.

A special thanks to Andrea, my father, who shot all the photos used in the projects of this book.

And last, a huge thanks to Francesca for the time she spent reading my drafts, trying the projects for the book, and giving me support during my long writing Sundays.

About the Reviewers

Berg Brandt is a well-rounded frontend engineer/web developer and a web designer with more than 12 years of experience in the Internet industry, specializing in designing, developing, and maintaining websites and web applications for different scales, markets, languages, and cultures.

Nowadays, Berg is the Engineering Team Leader of one of the Common User Experiences track of the Yahoo! Publishing Platform (YPP). The YPP empowers more than 300 high-traffic websites that reach millions of users across the globe every day. Berg is one of the project founders and the main author of the YPP CSS framework, one of its key components.

Angelos Evangelou is a web designer focused on creating templates. He obtained a degree in Web and Multimedia and has good knowledge of open source CMS platforms. He mainly loves to code and design websites from scratch, and as such, now focuses much of his time on template production.

> I would like to thank my parents and brothers. They have helped me have the confidence to pursue what I enjoy.

Andrew Wasson is a partner at Luna Design, a graphic design and web development studio in North Vancouver, British Columbia, Canada. Keenly interested in electronics and technology, Andrew built his first computer in high school and thus began his journey in computer programming, starting with machine language assemblers and then graduating to variations of Basic and C. Andrew has been developing and producing websites since 1998 and is active within the online community helping others master the finer points of website development. When he is not sharing the responsibilities of running their business with his wife Fiona, Andrew can be found riding or restoring his vintage ex-racing motorcycles.

www.PacktPub.com

Support files, eBooks, discount offers and more

You might want to visit www.PacktPub.com for support files and downloads related to your book.

Did you know that Packt offers eBook versions of every book published, with PDF and ePub files available? You can upgrade to the eBook version at www.PacktPub.com and as a print book customer, you are entitled to a discount on the eBook copy. Get in touch with us at service@packtpub.com for more details.

At www.PacktPub.com, you can also read a collection of free technical articles, sign up for a range of free newsletters and receive exclusive discounts and offers on Packt books and eBooks.

http://PacktLib.PacktPub.com

Do you need instant solutions to your IT questions? PacktLib is Packt's online digital book library. Here, you can access, read and search across Packt's entire library of books.

Why Subscribe?

- Fully searchable across every book published by Packt
- Copy and paste, print and bookmark content
- On demand and accessible via web browser

Free Access for Packt account holders

If you have an account with Packt at www.PacktPub.com, you can use this to access PacktLib today and view nine entirely free books. Simply use your login credentials for immediate access.

To Francesca, my parents, and Comparto Web.

Table of Contents

Preface

You'll be surprised, but CSS3 doesn't exist. Actually, this term is used to group a wide number of different specifications (see the the list at `http://www.w3.org/Style/CSS/current-work`), each of them with its own working team and completion state. Some are still Working Drafts while others are already Candidate Recommendations.

This book tries to present you with a snapshot of what can be done today with this technology. It is organized into 10 projects, each of them relying heavily on some of the new CSS features such as background gradients, Flexible Box Layout, or CSS filters.

All the projects have been developed and tested to work on the latest Chrome and Firefox browsers. The vast majority of them render and behave well even on Internet Explorer 10.

Wherever possible, a workaround to make things work even on older browsers is provided. In this way, different techniques and tools are introduced, such as feature detection with Modernizr, graceful degradation, fallback properties triggered with conditional comments, and a bunch of quality polyfill libraries.

The book also focuses on different kinds of tools, that are aimed at helping us while developing rather complex CSS documents. I'm talking about Sass and Compass, which provide us with a new syntax to better organize our project, and a bunch of useful functions that we'll see later in this book.

Dealing with vendor experimental prefixes is annoying. In this book, we'll discover how to use some libraries that do this task for us, either client or server side.

Well, there's nothing more to say here, I hope that you'll find the projects at least as interesting and fun to develop as I did, and that from them you'll learn new techniques, properties, and tools to help in your day-to-day job.

What this book covers

Chapter 1, No Sign Up? No Party!, will show you how to create a subscription form for your upcoming party. We use this chapter to discover how CSS3 features, such as some new pseudo-selectors, can enhance a form by adding specific styles to required fields or to valid/invalid ones.

Chapter 2, Shiny Buttons, will show you how to create some CSS3 enhanced buttons by using techniques such as rounded corners, multiple backgrounds, gradients, and shadows. Then we animate them using the classic `:hover` pseudo-selector with CSS3 transitions.

Chapter 3, Omni Menu, focuses on developing a menu that behaves differently according to the device we are using to view it. We achieve this goal using media queries and a nice feature detection library.

Chapter 4, Zooming User Interface, uses CSS3 transitions mixed with SVG graphics and the new `:target` pseudo-selector to create a fully functional zooming user interface that displays a cool infographic.

Chapter 5, An Image Gallery, will show you how to develop a pure CSS3 image slideshow with different transition effects such as fading, sliding and 3D rotation, and multiple navigation modes. Switching between different effects is made possible using the new `:checked` pseudo-selector. This chapter also introduces Sass, an extension of CSS3 that we can use to write cleaner, more readable, and smaller CSS files.

Chapter 6, Parallax Scrolling, focuses on building a real parallax effect triggered on page scroll. This is archived using 3D transform properties, such as `transform-style` and `perspective`.

Chapter 7, Video Killed the Radio Star, experiments with some cool video effects that can be archived using CSS3, including static and animated masks, blur, black and white, and so on. This chapter also deals with some interesting backward- and cross-browser compatibility issues.

Chapter 8, Go Go Gauges, shows how to take full advantage of the new CSS3 properties by creating an animated gauge that can be used as a widget in a webpage. This project also introduces the Compass: a Sass plugin that takes care of experimental prefixes, Reset stylesheet, and so on.

Chapter 9, Creating an Intro, takes CSS3 animations to another level by creating a 3D animation that uses a camera moving in a 3D scene.

Chapter 10, CSS Charting, will show you how to create bar charts and pie charts with CSS3 without the need for anything other than CSS and HTML. With the right polyfills we can then make these charts behave well even on older browsers.

What you need for this book

To develop the projects provided with this book you need a text editor (for example, Sublime Text 2, Notepad ++, and so on), and a web server to run the code. If you have never installed a web server, you may want to use a pre-packaged solution such as MAMP for Mac (`http://www.mamp.info/en/mamp/index.html`) or WampServer for Windows (`http://www.wampserver.com/`). These packages also install PHP and MySQL, that are not required to run the projects of this book, so you can simply ignore them.

Once you have downloaded, installed, and started the web server, you can create the projects within the web server's document root.

Who this book is for

This book is designed for frontend web developers. It requires a solid knowledge of CSS syntax and of the most common CSS2 properties and selectors.

Conventions

In this book, you will find a number of styles of text that distinguish between different kinds of information. Here are some examples of these styles, and an explanation of their meaning.

Code words in text are shown as follows: "We used the `:after` pseudo-selector to get access to the location just after the element with a `label` class."

A block of code is set as follows:

```
html{
    height: 100%;
    background: black;
    background-image: url('../img/background.jpg');
    background-repeat: no-repeat;
    background-size: cover;
    background-position: top left;
    font-family: sans-serif;
    color: #051a00;
}
```

When we wish to draw your attention to a particular part of a code block, the relevant lines or items are set in bold:

```
#old_panel{
  background: rgb(150,130,90);
  padding: 9px 0px 20px 0px;
}
```

Any command-line input or output is written as follows:

```
sass scss/application.scss:css/application.css
```

New terms and **important words** are shown in bold. Words that you see on the screen, in menus or dialog boxes for example, appear in the text like this: "Let's mark **border-radius**, **box-shadow**, **CSS Gradients**, and **multiple backgrounds**."

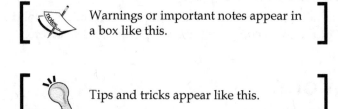

Warnings or important notes appear in a box like this.

Tips and tricks appear like this.

Reader feedback

Feedback from our readers is always welcome. Let us know what you think about this book—what you liked or may have disliked. Reader feedback is important for us to develop titles that you really get the most out of.

To send us general feedback, simply send an e-mail to feedback@packtpub.com, and mention the book title via the subject of your message.

If there is a topic that you have expertise in and you are interested in either writing or contributing to a book, see our author guide on www.packtpub.com/authors.

Customer support

Now that you are the proud owner of a Packt book, we have a number of things to help you to get the most from your purchase.

Downloading the example code

You can download the example code files for all Packt books you have purchased from your account at http://www.PacktPub.com. If you purchased this book elsewhere, you can visit http://www.PacktPub.com/support and register to have the files e-mailed directly to you.

Errata

Although we have taken every care to ensure the accuracy of our content, mistakes do happen. If you find a mistake in one of our books—maybe a mistake in the text or the code—we would be grateful if you would report this to us. By doing so, you can save other readers from frustration and help us improve subsequent versions of this book. If you find any errata, please report them by visiting http://www.packtpub. com/support, selecting your book, clicking on the **errata submission form** link, and entering the details of your errata. Once your errata are verified, your submission will be accepted and the errata will be uploaded on our website, or added to any list of existing errata, under the Errata section of that title. Any existing errata can be viewed by selecting your title from http://www.packtpub.com/support.

Piracy

Piracy of copyright material on the Internet is an ongoing problem across all media. At Packt, we take the protection of our copyright and licenses very seriously. If you come across any illegal copies of our works, in any form, on the Internet, please provide us with the location address or website name immediately so that we can pursue a remedy.

Please contact us at copyright@packtpub.com with a link to the suspected pirated material.

We appreciate your help in protecting our authors, and our ability to bring you valuable content.

Questions

You can contact us at questions@packtpub.com if you are having a problem with any aspect of the book, and we will do our best to address it.

1
No Sign Up? No Party!

CSS3 has been a big leap forward for forms. Not only are new style possibilities available, but new and powerful pseudo-selectors can also now be used to modify the appearance of our page, depending on the state of the form or of its fields. In this chapter, we will use a party registration form as a test case to show how this component can be enhanced by the new CSS specifications. We will also pay attention to how we can retain the right behavior for older browsers. We're going to cover the following topics:

- HTML structure
- The form
- Basic styling
- Marking required fields
- The checked radio buttons trick
- Counting invalid fields
- Balloon styling

HTML structure

Let's start with some HTML5 code to shape the structure of our project's web page. To do so, create a file, named `index.html`, in a new folder, named `no_signup_no_party`, containing the following markup:

```html
<!doctype html>
<html>
<head>
  <meta charset="utf-8">
  <meta http-equiv="X-UA-Compatible" content="IE=edge"/>
  <title>No signup? No party!</title>
  <link rel="stylesheet" type="text/css"
href="http://yui.yahooapis.com/3.7.3/build/cssreset/cssreset-
min.css">
  <link rel='stylesheet' type='text/css'
href='http://fonts.googleapis.com/css?family=Port+Lligat+Sans'>
  <link rel='stylesheet' type='text/css'
href='css/application.css'>
  <script
src="http://html5shiv.googlecode.com/svn/trunk/html5.js">
</script>
</head>
<body>
  <article>
    <header>
      <h1>No signup? No party!</h1>
      <p>
        Would you like to join the most amazing party of the
planet? Fill out this form with your info but.. hurry up! only a
few tickets are still available!
      </p>
    </header>
    <form name="subscription">
      <!-- FORM FIELDS -->
      <input type="submit" value="Yep! Count me in!">
    </form>
    <footer>
      Party will be held at Nottingham Arena next sunday, for info
call 555-192-132 or drop us a line at info@nottinghamparties.fun
    </footer>
  </article>
</body>
</html>
```

Downloading the example code

You can download the example code files for all Packt books you have purchased through your account at `http://www.packtpub.com`. If you purchased this book elsewhere, you can visit `http://www.packtpub.com/support` and register to have the files e-mailed directly to you.

As you can see from the markup, we are taking advantage of the new structure offered by HTML5. Tags such as `<article>`, `<header>`, and `<footer>` enrich the page by adding semantic meaning to the content. These tags are rendered exactly as `<div>` but are, semantically speaking, better because they explain something about their content.

For more information, I suggest you look at the following article: `http://html5doctor.com/lets-talk-about-semantics`

Flavor text aside, the only section that needs detailed explanation is the `<head>` section. Within this tag, we ask the browser to include some external assets that will help us along the way.

Reset stylesheet and custom fonts

First, there is a Reset stylesheet, which is particularly useful for ensuring that all the CSS properties that browsers apply by default to HTML elements get removed. In this project, we use the one offered freely by Yahoo!, which basically sets all the properties to `none` or something equivalent.

Next, we ask for another stylesheet. This one is from a Google service called Google Web Fonts (`www.google.com/webfonts`), which distributes fonts that can be embedded and used within a web page. Custom web fonts are defined with a special `@font-face` property that contains the link to the font file the browser has to implement.

```
@font-face{
  font-family: YourFontName;
  src: url('yourfonturl.eot');
}
```

Unfortunately, to reach the maximum possible compatibility between browsers, more font file formats are required, and so a more complex statement is necessary. The following statements help achieve such compatibility:

```
@font-face{
  font-family: YourFontName;
  src: url('yourfonturl.eot');
  src:
    url('yourfonturl.woff') format('woff'),
    url('yourfonturl.ttf') format('truetype'),
    url('yourfonturl.svg') format('svg');
  font-weight: normal;
  font-style: normal;
}
```

Google Web Fonts provides us with a stylesheet containing these statements for the fonts we choose, saving us all the trouble related to font conversion.

Next, let's create an empty file for our stylesheet under a `css` folder within the project.

Last but not least, we need to ensure that even older Internet Explorer browsers will be able to handle the new HTML5 tags correctly. `html5shiv` (`html5shiv. googlecode.com`) is a small JavaScript file that accomplishes exactly this task.

Creating the form

Now let's write the HTML code for the form by adding the following code below the `<!--FORM FIELDS-->` mark:

```
<fieldset>
  <legend>
    Some info about you:
  </legend>
  <input type="text" name="name" id="name" placeholder="e.g.
Sandro" title="Your name, required" required>
  <label class="label" for="name"> Name: </label>
  <input type="text" name="surname" id="surname" placeholder="e.g.
Paganotti" title="Your surname, required" required>
  <label class="label" for="surname"> Surname: </label>
  <input type="email" name="email" id="email" placeholder="e.g.
sandro.paganotti@gmail.com" title="Your email address, a valid
email is required" required>
  <label class="label" for="email"> E-mail: </label>
  <input type="text" name="twitter" id="twitter" placeholder="e.g.
@sandropaganotti" title="Your twitter username, starting with @"
pattern="@[a-zA-Z0-9]+">
```

```
    <label class="label" for="twitter"> Twitter:</label>
    <footer></footer>
</fieldset>
```

HTML5 offers some new attributes that we will explore briefly, as follows:

- `placeholder`: This is used to specify some help text that is displayed within the field when empty.

- `required`: This is used to mark the field as required. It's a Boolean attribute that tells the browser to ensure that the field is not empty before submitting the form. This attribute is part of the new form validation features, which basically offer a way to specify some input constraints on the client side. Unfortunately, each browser handles the display of the error messages contained in the `title` attribute in a different way, but we'll check this later in the chapter.

- `pattern`: This is a powerful and sometimes complex way of specifying a validation pattern. It needs a regular expression as a value. This expression is then checked against the data inserted by the user. In case of failure, the message contained in the `title` attribute is displayed.

  In the given example, the pattern value is `@[a-zA-Z0-9]+`, which means "one or more occurrences (the + sign) of glyphs from the ranges `a-z` (all lowercase letters), `A-Z` (all uppercase letters), and `0-9` (all digits)".

 More ready-to-use patterns can be found at
`http://html5pattern.com/`.

Like most of the features introduced by HTML5, even new form attributes such as the ones we saw in the code earlier suffer in terms of complete browser compatibility.

To get a glimpse of the current browser support for these attributes and many other HTML5 and CSS3 features, I suggest going to `http://caniuse.com/`.

Misplaced labels

There's another oddity in this code: labels are placed after the fields they're linked to. This markup, although uncommon, is still valid and gives us some new interesting options to intercept user interaction with the form elements. This may sound mysterious, but we're going to analyze the technique in detail in a few pages from now.

Let's add another `fieldset` element below the one we just wrote:

```
<fieldset class="preferences">
  <legend> Your party preferences: </legend>
  <input type="radio" name="beers" id="4_beers" value="4">
  <label class="beers" for="4_beers">4 beers</label>
  <input type="radio" name="beers" id="3_beers" value="3">
  <label class="beers" for="3_beers">3 beers</label>
  <input type="radio" name="beers" id="2_beers" value="2">
  <label class="beers" for="2_beers">2 beers</label>
  <input type="radio" name="beers" id="1_beers" value="1">
  <label class="beers" for="1_beers">1 beers</label>
  <input type="radio" name="beers" id="0_beers" value="0"
required>
  <label class="beers" for="0_beers">0 beers</label>
  <span  class="label"> How many beers?: </span>
  <input type="radio" name="chips" id="4_chips" value="4">
  <label class="chips" for="4_chips">4 chips</label>
  <input type="radio" name="chips" id="3_chips" value="3">
  <label class="chips" for="3_chips">3 chips</label>
  <input type="radio" name="chips" id="2_chips" value="2">
  <label class="chips" for="2_chips">2 chips</label>
  <input type="radio" name="chips" id="1_chips" value="1">
  <label class="chips" for="1_chips">1 chips</label>
  <input type="radio" name="chips" id="0_chips" value="0"
required>
  <label class="chips" for="0_chips">0 chips</label>
  <span class="label"> How many chips?: </span>
  <footer></footer>
</fieldset>
```

Nothing to highlight here; we've just added two radio button groups. Now, if we try to run what we've done up to now in a browser, we are going to face some disappointment because the default browser's styles have been removed by the Reset stylesheet.

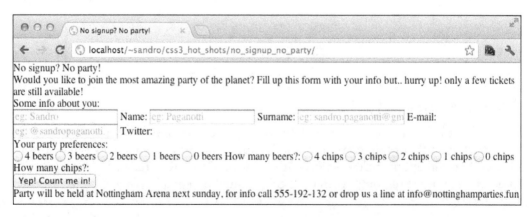

Time to add some basic styling!

Basic styling

What we need to do is center the form, give the right size to the texts, choose a background, and adjust the displacement of labels and fields.

Let's start with the background. What we want to achieve is to place an image as big as possible to fit the page while keeping its proportions. This simple task in the "CSS2 era" would involve some use of JavaScript, such as the well-known Redux jQuery plugin (`http://bavotasan.com/2011/full-sizebackground-image-jquery-plugin/`). With CSS3 it's just a matter of a few statements:

```
html{
   height: 100%;
   background: black;
   background-image: url('../img/background.jpg');
   background-repeat: no-repeat;
   background-size: cover;
   background-position: top left;
   font-family: sans-serif;
   color: #051a00;
}
```

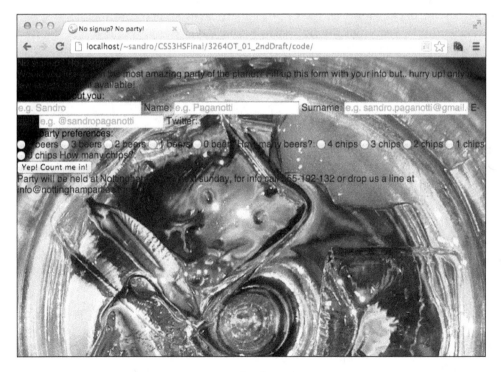

What does the trick here is the `background-size` property, which accepts the following values:

- `length`: Using this value, we can express the size of the background using any units of measurement, for example `background-size: 10px 10px;`.

- `percentage`: Using this value, we can specify a background size that varies with the size of the element, for example `background-size: 10% 10%;`.

- `cover`: This value scales the image (without stretching it) to cover the whole area of the element. This means that part of the image may not be visible because it could get bigger than the container.

- `contain`: This value scales the image (without stretching it) to the maximum size available while keeping the whole image within the container. This, obviously, could leave some area of the element uncovered.

So, by using `cover`, we ensure that the whole page will be covered by our image, but we can do more! If we run all that we've done up to here in a browser, we will see that the pixels of our background image become visible if we enlarge the window too much. To avoid this, what we can do is to use another background image on top of this one. We can use small black dots to hide the pixels of the underlying image and achieve a better result.

The good news is that we can do this without using another element, as CSS3 allows more than one background on the same element. We can use commas (,) to separate the backgrounds, keeping in mind that what we declare first will lay over the others. So, let's change the preceding code a bit:

```
html{
    height: 100%;
    background: black;
    background-image:
        url('../img/dots.png'),
        url('../img/background.jpg');
    background-repeat: repeat, no-repeat;
    background-size: auto, cover;
    background-position: center center, top left;
    font-family: sans-serif;
    color: #051a00;
}
```

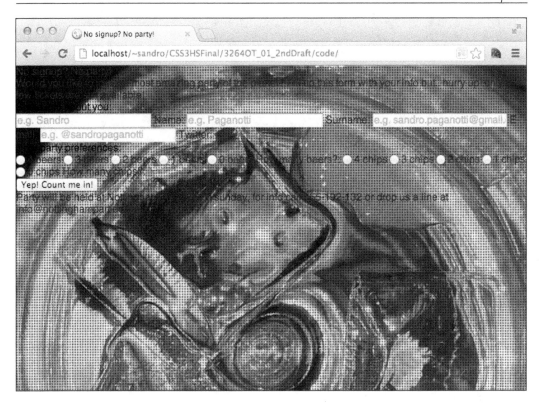

Also, all the other background-related properties act in the same way. If we omit one of the values, the previous one is used, so writing `background-repeat: repeat` is the same as writing `background-repeat: repeat, repeat` if two background images are declared.

Defining properties

Let's move on and define the rest of the required properties to complete the first phase of the project:

```
/* the main container */
article{
  width: 600px;
  margin: 0 auto;
  background: #6cbf00;
  border: 10px solid white;
  margin-top: 80px;
  position: relative;
  padding: 30px;
  border-radius: 20px;
}
```

```css
/* move the title over the main container */
article h1{
  width: 600px;
  text-align: center;
  position: absolute;
  top: -62px;
/* using the custom font family provided by google */
  font-family: 'Port Lligat Sans', cursive;
  color: white;
  font-size: 60px;
  text-transform: uppercase;
}

/* the small text paragraphs */
article p,
article > footer{
  padding-bottom: 1em;
  line-height: 1.4em;
}

/* the fieldsets' legends */
article legend{
  font-family: 'Port Lligat Sans', cursive;
  display: block;
  color: white;
  font-size: 25px;
  padding-bottom: 10px;
}

.label{
  display: block;
  float: left;
  clear: left;
}

/* positioning the submit button */
input[type=submit]{
  display:block;
  width: 200px;
  margin: 20px auto;
}

/* align texts input on the right */
input[type=text], input[type=email]{
  float: right;
  clear: right;
  width: 350px;
  border: none;
  padding-left: 5px;
}
```

```
input[type=text],
input[type=email],
.label{
  margin: 2px 0px 2px 20px;
  line-height: 30px;
  height: 30px;
}

span + input[type=radio], legend + input[type=radio]{
  clear: right
}

/* size of the small labels linked to each radio */
.preferences label.chips,
.preferences label.beers{
  width: 60px;
  background-image: none;
}

input[type="radio"]{
  padding-right: 4px;
}

input[type="radio"],
.preferences label{
  float: right;
  line-height: 30px;
  height: 30px;
}
```

There are just a few things to underline here. First of all, by using some floats, we've moved all the fields to the right and the labels to the left. Next, we've defined some distance between the elements. Maybe the most cryptic statement is the following one:

```
span + input[type=radio], legend + input[type=radio]{
  clear: right
}
```

Due to the floating that we just talked about, the first element of each group of radio buttons became the rightmost. So, we identify this element by using the `selector1 + selector2` selector, which indicates that the specified elements must be siblings. This is called an **adjacent sibling selector**, and selects all the elements matching the `selector2` selector that directly follows an element matching the `selector1` selector. Finally, using `clear:right` we simply state that there must be no other floating elements to the right of these radio buttons.

Let's reload the project in the browser to appreciate the result of our work:

Marking required fields

Let's look at an easy trick to automatically display an asterisk (*) near the labels of required fields. The HTML5 form validation model introduces some new and very interesting pseudo-selectors:

- :valid: It matches only fields that are in a valid state.

- :invalid: It works in the opposite way, matching only fields with errors. This includes empty fields with the required attribute set to true.

- :required: It matches only fields with the required flag, whether they're filled or not.

- :optional: It works with all fields the without the required flag.

In our case, we need to match all the labels that follow a field that has the `required` attribute. Now the HTML5 structure we implemented earlier comes in handy because we can take advantage of the + selector to accomplish this.

```
input:required + .label:after, input:required + * + .label:after{
  content: '*';
}
```

We added a small variation (`input:required + * + .label:after`) in order to intercept the structure of the radio buttons as well.

Let's analyze the sentence a bit before moving on. We used the `:after` pseudo-selector to get access to the location just after the element with a `label` class. Then, with the `content` property, we injected the asterisk within that location.

If we reload the page we can verify that, now, all the labels that belong to fields with a `required` flag end with an asterisk. Someone may point out that screen readers do not recognize this technique. To find a way around this, we can take advantage of the `aria-required` property, part of the WAI-ARIA specification (`http://www.w3.org/TR/WCAG20-TECHS/ARIA2`).

The checked radio buttons trick

Now we can concentrate on the radio buttons, but how can we render them in a better way? There is a cool technique for this; it takes advantage of the fact that you can check a radio button even by clicking on its linked label. What we can do is hide the input elements and style the corresponding labels, maybe using icons that represent chips and beers.

Let's begin by removing the text from the radio button labels and changing the cursor appearance when it's hovering over them:

```css
.preferences label{
  float: right;
  text-indent: -100px;
  width: 40px !important;
  line-height: normal;
  height: 30px;
  overflow: hidden;
   cursor: pointer;
}
```

Well done! Now we have to hide the radio buttons. We can achieve this by placing a patch with the same color as the background over the radio button. Let's do that:

```css
input[type=radio]{
  position: absolute;
  right: 30px;
  margin-top: 10px;
}

input[type=radio][name=chips]{
  margin-top: 35px;
}

span + input[type=radio] + label,
legend + input[type=radio] + label{
  clear: right;
  margin-right: 80px;
  counter-reset: checkbox;
}

.preferences input[type="radio"]:required + label:after{
  content: '';
  position: absolute;
  right: 25px;
```

```
    min-height: 10px;
    margin-top: -22px;
    text-align: right;
    background: #6cbf00;
    padding: 10px 10px;
    display: block;
}
```

If we now try to submit the form either using WebKit-based browsers or Firefox, we can appreciate that the validation balloons related to radio buttons are displayed correctly on both of them.

Displaying icons within radio button labels

Let's move on and work on the radio button labels that, at the moment, are completely empty because we moved the text away using the text-indent property. What we are going to do now is to put a tiny placeholder image within each label, and by taking advantage of the CSS3 ~ selector, create a pseudo-star rating system with a nice mouse-over effect.

Due to the fact that we have to work with different images (for beers and chips), we have to duplicate some statements. Let's start with the .beers labels:

```
.preferences label.beers{
  background: transparent url('../img/beer_not_selected.png')
no-repeat center center;
}

.preferences label.beers:hover ~ label.beers,
.preferences label.beers:hover,
.preferences input[type=radio][name=beers]:checked ~ label.beers{
  background-image: url('../img/beer.png');
  counter-increment: checkbox;
}
```

The elem1 ~ elem2 selector applies to all the elem2 labels that are siblings of the elem1 label and that follow it (the elem2 labels don't have to be adjacent, though). This way, we can target all the labels that follow a label that is in the hover state (when the mouse is over the element) with the selector .preferences label.beers:hover ~ label.beers.

Using the CSS3 :checked pseudo-class selector, we can identify the radio button that has been checked, and by applying the same trick that we just discussed, we can target all the labels that follow a checked radio button by using .preferences input[type=radio][name=beers]:checked ~ label.beers. By putting together these two selectors and a classic .preferences label. beers:hover selector, we are now able to change the placeholder image reflecting the user interaction with the radio buttons. Now let's add a final cool feature. We have used the counter-increment property to keep track of the number of selected labels, so we can take advantage of this counter and display it.

```
.preferences input[type=radio][name=beers]:required +
label.beers:after{
   content: counter(checkbox) " beers!";
}
```

Let's try the result in a browser:

Now, we have to duplicate the same statements for the `.chips` labels too:

```css
.preferences label.chips{
  background: transparent
url('../img/frenchfries_not_selected.png')
no-repeat center center;
}

.preferences label.chips:hover ~ label.chips,
.preferences label.chips:hover,
.preferences input[type=radio][name=chips]:checked ~ label.chips {
 background-image: url('../img/frenchfries.png');
  counter-increment: checkbox;
}

.preferences input[type=radio][name=chips]:required +
label.chips:after {
  content: counter(checkbox) " chips!";
}
```

All of the styling we did in this chapter has one big problem; if the browser doesn't support CSS3, it successfully hides both radio buttons and text labels but fails to add their image replacements, making everything unusable. There are a few ways to prevent this. The one introduced here is to use **media queries**.

Media queries, which will be covered in detail in a later project, basically consist of a statement that describes some conditions required to apply some styles. Let's consider the following example:

```css
@media all and (max-width: 1000px){
  body{
    background: red;
  }
}
```

In this example, the body background is turned into red only if the size of the browser window doesn't exceed `1000px`. Media queries are really useful to apply specific styles only to target devices (smartphones, tablets, and so on), but they have another interesting property; if a browser supports them, it also supports the CSS3 rules we used, so we can place all of the CSS written in this and in the previous sections within a media query statement:

```css
@media all and (min-device-width: 1024px){

/* --- all of this and previous sections' statements --- */

}
```

With this trick, we solved another subtle problem. Trying the project on an iPad without this media query statement would have resulted in some problems with clicking on the radio buttons. This is because labels do not respond to clicks on iOS. By implementing this media query, we force iOS devices to fall back to regular radio buttons.

Counting and displaying invalid fields

In the previous section, we used some properties without explaining them; they are `counter-reset` and `counter-increment`. Plus, we used a function-like command called `counter()`. In this section, we'll explain these properties by creating a mechanism to display the number of invalid fields. A **counter** is basically a variable we can name and whose value can be incremented using `counter-increment`. Next, this counter can be displayed by using the `counter(variable name)` declaration within a `content` property.

Let's see a small example:

```
<ul>
    <li>element</li>
    <li>element</li>
    <li>element</li>
</ul>
<p></p>

<style>

ul{
    counter-reset: elements;
}

li{
    counter-increment: elements;
}

p:after{
    content: counter(elements) ' elements';
}

</style>
```

Trying this small bit of code results in a p element containing the sentence
3 elements:

We can combine these powerful properties with the new form pseudo-selector to
obtain a way to display valid and invalid fields.

Implementing the counters

Let's start by creating two counters, invalid and fields, and resetting them at each
fieldset element because we want to display the invalid fields for each fieldset
element. Then, we increment both counters when we find an invalid field and only
the fields counter when we find a valid field.

```
fieldset{
  counter-reset: invalid fields;
}

input:not([type=submit]):not([type=radio]):invalid,
input[type=radio]:required:invalid{
  counter-increment: invalid fields;
  border-left: 5px solid #ff4900;
}

input:not([type=submit]):not([type=radio]):valid,
input[type=radio]:required{
  counter-increment: fields;
  border-left: 5px solid #116300;
}
```

The :not pseudo-selector is pretty straightforward. It subtracts the elements
matching the selector within the parentheses from the elements matching the
leftmost selector. If this seems a bit confusing, let's try to read the last selector: match
all the input elements, whose type value is *not* submit and *not* radio, that respond
to the :valid pseudo-selector.

Almost there! Now that we have the counters, let's display them using the `footer` element we have:

```css
fieldset footer{
  clear: both;
  position: relative;
}

fieldset:not([fake]) footer:after{
  content: 'yay, section completed, move on!';
  text-align: right;
  display: block;
  font-size: 13px;
  padding-top: 10px;
}

/* the value of the content property must be on one single line */
fieldset > input:invalid ~ footer:after{
  content: counter(invalid) '/' counter(fields) " fields with
problems; move the mouse over the fields with red marks to see
details.\a Fields with * are required.";
  white-space: pre;
}
```

The `:not([fake])` selector is used like the media query shown earlier. We just want to ensure that only the browsers that support the `:valid` and `:invalid` pseudo-selectors can interpret this selector.

This last addition has some drawbacks, though; mixing presentation with content is generally something to avoid.

Balloon styling

Each browser actually displays form errors in its own way, and we can't do very much to affect this visualization. The only exceptions are WebKit-based browsers, which let us change the appearance of such messages. The following code shows how an error balloon is constructed in these browsers:

```html
<div>::-webkit-validation-bubble
  <div>::-webkit-validation-bubble-arrow-clipper
    <div>::-webkit-validation-bubble-arrow
    </div>
  </div>::-webkit-validation-bubble-message
  <div>
```

```
        <b>Browser validation message</b>
        element's title attribute
    </div>
</div>
```

We can access all the elements that compose an error message by using the special pseudo-classes listed in the preceding code. So, let's begin!

```
::-webkit-validation-bubble{
  margin-left: 380px;
  margin-top: -50px;
  width: 200px;
}

input[type=radio]::-webkit-validation-bubble{
  margin-left: 50px;
  margin-top: -50px;
}

::-webkit-validation-bubble-arrow-clipper{
  -webkit-transform: rotate(270deg) translateY(-104px)
translateX(40px);
}

::-webkit-validation-bubble-arrow{
  background: #000;
  border: none;
  box-shadow: 0px 0px 10px rgba(33,33,33,0.8);
}

::-webkit-validation-bubble-message{
  border: 5px solid black;
  background-image: none;
  box-shadow: 0px 0px 10px rgba(33,33,33,0.8);
}
```

With -webkit-transform, we're applying some transformation to the matched elements. In this case, we're moving the arrow, which usually lies on the bottom of the balloon, to the left side of it.

The following is a glimpse of how our completed project looks:

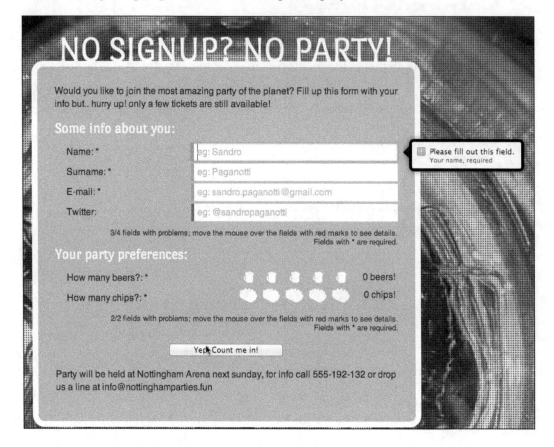

Graceful degradation

As we might expect, this project is not fully supported on all browsers because it implements HTML5 and CSS3 features that, of course, aren't included in old browsers. Many techniques exist to find a way around this issue; the one we'll look at now is called **graceful degradation**. It basically focuses on making the core functionalities of the project as widely supported as possible while accepting that everything else might be unsupported and thus not displayed.

Our project is a good example of graceful degradation: when a browser does not support a specific property, its effects are simply ignored without affecting the basic functionality of the form.

To prove this, let's try the project on IE8, which basically has no CSS3 support:

To achieve the best possible browser support, we may also want to hide footer elements and radio buttons on IE9 because, otherwise, they'll be displayed but they won't behave as expected. To do so, we need to add a conditional comment in our index.html file, just before the end of the head section. We'll see in the later chapters how conditional comments work, but for now let's say that they allow us to specify some markup that needs to be interpreted only by chosen browsers.

```
<!--[if IE 9]>
  <style>
    footer, input[name=beers], input[name=chips]{
      display: none;
    }
  </style>
<![endif]-->
```

Summary

In this first project, we've explored how CSS3 can enhance our forms with useful information derived from the markup and the status of the fields. In the next chapter, we'll focus our attention on buttons and how we can mimic real-world shapes and behavior without using images by taking full advantage of gradients and other CSS3 properties.

2
Shiny Buttons

CSS3 buttons have been considered a hot topic since they were first introduced on cutting-edge browsers' nightly builds. Buttons are important, well-recognized elements of the majority of user interfaces. What makes them a hot topic for web developers is that CSS3 buttons are easy to modify by simply changing the text or the stylesheet declarations.

In this chapter, we'll create buttons that mimic their real-world counterparts using only CSS3. While doing so, we'll explore new CSS properties and tricks to achieve our goals. We will cover the following topics:

- A coin-operated push button
- The `:before` and `:after` pseudo-selectors
- Gradients
- Avoiding experimental prefixes
- Shadows
- Adding labels
- Handling mouse clicks
- Small change in CSS, big results
- An ON/OFF switch
- The active state
- The checked state
- Adding colors
- Supporting older browsers
- A final note on CSS gradient syntax

Creating a coin-operated push button

In the first part of this chapter we focus on creating a realistic coin-operated push button. We want to use as much CSS as possible and to take advantage of the new features without using images. The following screenshot is a glimpse of the result:

To start with, let's create a folder called `shiny_buttons`, where we'll store all of the project's files. Then, we need a file, `index.html`, filled with very little markup:

```
<!doctype html>
<html>
<head>
  <meta http-equiv="X-UA-Compatible" content="IE=edge"/>
  <meta charset="utf-8">
  <title>Shiny Buttons: from the reality to the web!</title>
  <link
href='http://fonts.googleapis.com/css?family=Chango|Frijole|
Alegreya+SC:700' rel='stylesheet' type='text/css'>
  <link rel="stylesheet" type="text/css"
href="http://yui.yahooapis.com/3.4.1/build/cssreset/cssreset-min.css">
  <link rel="stylesheet" type="text/css"
href="css/application.css">
  <script
src="http://html5shiv.googlecode.com/svn/trunk/html5.js"></script>
</head>
<body>
  <section>
```

```
<article id="arcade_game">
  <a href="#" role="button" class="punch">punch</a>
  <a href="#" role="button" class="jump">jump</a>
</article>

  </section>
</body>
</html>
```

As the markup shows, we are using a single `<a>` element to declare our button. An anchor tag may not seem sophisticated enough to produce a complex button and leads us to believe that we'll need more HTML, but this is not the case. We can achieve amazing results using only this tag, along with our CSS3 declarations.

The :before and :after pseudo-selectors

As we discovered in the previous chapter, pseudo-selectors can be treated as elements and styled without the need to add additional markup to the HTML page. If we set the `<a>` element to `position:relative`, and both `:after` and `:before` to `position:absolute`, we can place them using coordinates relative to the position of `<a>`. Let's try this by creating an `application.css` file in a `css` folder within the project:

```css
/* link */
#arcade_game a{
  display: block;
  position: relative;
  text-transform: uppercase;
  line-height: 100px;
  text-decoration: none;
  font-family: 'Frijole', cursive;
  font-size: 40px;
  width: 300px;
  padding: 10px 0px 10px 120px;
  margin: 0px auto;
  color: rgb(123,26,55);
}

/* :before and :after setup */
#arcade_game a:before,
#arcade_game a:after{
  content: "";
  display: block;
  position: absolute;
```

```
    left: 0px;
    top: 50%;
}

/* :before */
#arcade_game a:before{
  z-index: 2;
  width: 70px;
  height: 70px;
  line-height: 70px;
  left: 15px;
  margin-top: -35px;
  border-radius: 35px;
  background-color: red; /* to be removed */
}

/* :after */
#arcade_game a:after{
  z-index: 1;
  width: 100px;
  height: 100px;
  border-radius: 50px;
  margin-top: -50px;
  background-color: green; /* to be removed */
}
```

If we load what we've done so far in a browser, we start noticing the shape of a coin-op push button. Two circles, one within the other, positioned to the left of the label, as shown in the following screenshot:

All we did to create the circle shape was to impose a border radius equal to half the size of the box. Well done! Now we can remove the green and red circle backgrounds and move on to explore gradients.

Gradients

When using CSS gradients, we instruct the browser's layout engine to draw patterns following our CSS directions. A **gradient** corresponds to a runtime-generated, size-independent image, and so it can be used wherever the `url()` notation is allowed. There are four types of gradients: `linear-gradient`, `repeating-linear-gradient`, `radial-gradient`, and `repeating-radial-gradient`. The following gradient code example provides an introductory overview of each of them:

```
<!doctype html>
<html>
<head>
  <meta charset="utf8">
  <title>Explore gradients</title>

  <style>
    .box{
      width: 400px;
      height: 80px;
      border: 3px solid rgb(60,60,60);
      margin: 10px auto;
      border-radius: 5px;
      font-size: 30px;
      text-shadow: 2px 2px white;
    }

    #linear{
      background-image: linear-gradient(top left, red, white,
green);
    }

    #repeating_linear{
      background-image: repeating-linear-gradient(top left, red,
white, red 30%);
    }

    #radial{
      background-image: radial-gradient(center center, ellipse
cover, white, blue);
    }
```

```
    #repeating_radial{
       background-image: repeating-radial-gradient(center center,
ellipse cover, white, blue, white 30px);
       }

    #collapsed_linear{
       background-image: linear-gradient(left, red, red 33%, white
33%, white 66%, green 66%);
       }

    #collapsed_radial{
       background-image: radial-gradient(center center, ellipse
contain, white, white 55%, blue 55%);
       }

  </style>

</head>
<body>
  <section>

    <div id="linear" class="box">linear</div>
    <div id="repeating_linear" class="box">repeating_linear</div>
    <div id="radial" class="box">radial</div>
    <div id="repeating_radial" class="box">repeating_radial</div>
    <div id="collapsed_linear" class="box">collapsed_linear</div>
    <div id="collapsed_radial" class="box">collapsed_radial</div>

  </section>
</body>
</html>
```

The gradient syntax

In the preceding gradient code example, it is clear that each statement contains positional information (for example, `top left` or `45deg`) with color steps, which can optionally have a value indicating where the color is to stop. If two colors stop at exactly the same position, we obtain a sharp color change instead of a gradient.

Extra parameters are allowed for radial gradients. In particular, we can choose the shape of the gradient, between circle and ellipsis, and how the gradient fills the element's area. To specify, we can choose among the following options:

- `closest-side`: With this parameter, the gradient expands until it meets the closest side of the containing element
- `closest-corner`: With this parameter, the gradient expands until it meets the closest corner of the containing element
- `farthest-side`: With this parameter, the gradients expands until it meets the farthest side of the containing element
- `farthest-corner`: With this parameter, the gradients expands until it meets the farthest corner of the containing element
- `contain`: This is an alias to `closest-side`
- `cover`: This is an alias to `farthest-corner`

The following screenshot shows the result of the preceding code executed in a browser:

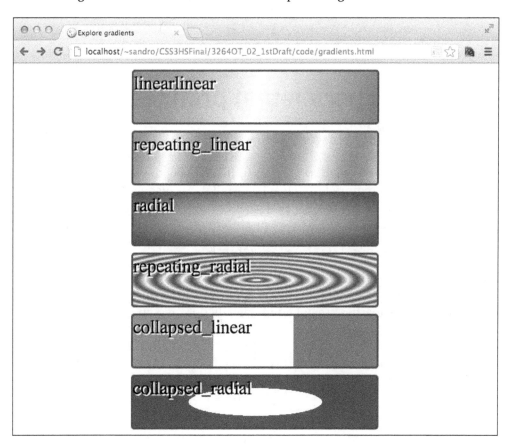

Unfortunately, the previous screenshot does not illustrate what we see if we run the example code in a web browser. As a matter of fact, if we execute the previous code in a browser supporting CSS3 gradients, such as Google Chrome, what we obtain is a list of white boxes with black borders. This is because gradients are considered experimental and thus need to be prefixed with a browser-specific string for every browser we want to support (for example, `-webkit-`, `-ms-`, `-o-`, and `-moz-`). This means that we have to duplicate the statement for each browser we'd like to support. For example, in the `#linear` selector from the previous code, to achieve the maximum compatibility, we should have written:

```
#linear{
    background-image: -webkit-linear-gradient(top left, red, white,
green);
    background-image: -ms-linear-gradient(top left, red, white,
green);
    background-image: -o-linear-gradient(top left, red, white,
green);
    background-image: -moz-linear-gradient(top left, red, white,
green);
    background-image: linear-gradient(top left, red, white, green);
}
```

Avoiding experimental prefixes

We need to find a way to avoid writing a lot of duplicated CSS code only to implement all the existing browser experimental prefixes. A good solution is provided by Prefix Free (`http://leaverou.github.com/prefixfree/`), a small JavaScript library created by Lea Verou that detects the user's browser and dynamically adds the required prefixes. To install it, we just need to download the `.js` file in a `js` folder within our project, name it `prefixfree.js`, and add the corresponding script tag to `index.html` just after the `css` request:

```
<script src="js/prefixfree.js"></script>
```

From this point on, we don't have to worry about prefixes anymore because this library will do the heavy lifting for us. There are, however, some minor drawbacks; some properties are not automatically detected and prefixed (for example, `radial-gradient` and `repeating-radial-gradient` are not prefixed with `-moz-`) and we have to suffer a brief delay, roughly equal to the script download time, before the CSS gets correctly prefixed.

So, let's move on and add some gradients to our push buttons:

```
#arcade_game a:before, #arcade_game a:after{
  background: gray;   /* to be removed */
}


#arcade_game a:before{
  background-image:
    -moz-radial-gradient(7px 7px, ellipse farthest-side,
    rgba(255,255,255,0.8), rgba(255,255,255,0.6) 3px,
    rgba(200,200,200,0.0) 20px);
  background-image:
    radial-gradient(7px 7px, ellipse farthest-side,
    rgba(255,255,255,0.8), rgba(255,255,255,0.6) 3px,
    rgba(200,200,200,0.0) 20px);
}


#arcade_game a:after{
  background-image:
    -moz-radial-gradient(7px 7px, ellipse farthest-side,
    rgba(255,255,255,0.8), rgba(255,255,255,0.6) 3px,
    rgba(200,200,200,0.0) 20px),
    -moz-radial-gradient(50px 50px, rgba(255,255,255,0),
    rgba(255,255,255,0) 40px, rgba(200,200,200,0.1) 43px,
    rgba(255,255,255,0.0) 50px);
  background-image:
    radial-gradient(7px 7px, ellipse farthest-side,
    rgba(255,255,255,0.8), rgba(255,255,255,0.6) 3px,
    rgba(200,200,200,0.0) 20px),
    radial-gradient(50px 50px, rgba(255,255,255,0),
    rgba(255,255,255,0) 40px, rgba(200,200,200,0.1) 43px,
    rgba(255,255,255,0.0) 50px);
}
```

In order to focus specifically on the subject of adding new features to our buttons, the preceding code does not repeat the existing CSS declarations from application. css. It doesn't matter how we apply the new instructions; we can either append the previous statements or merge the properties of each selector. In any case, the results will be the same.

With the previous code, we created two light points, using radial gradients to simulate the shape and the reflection of our push button. CSS3 allows us to create this effect by supporting the rgba() notation, which accepts an alpha value between 0 (transparent) and 1 (opaque).

Let's try the result in the browser:

Upcoming syntax changes for CSS3 gradients

The latest editor draft about CSS3 gradients (http://www.w3.org/TR/2012/
CR-css3-images-20120417/) introduced a small syntax change when providing
keywords to define positional information. So, instead of writing:

```
linear-gradient(bottom, blue, red);
```

We now need to write:

```
linear-gradient(to top, blue, red);
```

For the radial gradient syntax there are a few more changes; so what we
wrote earlier:

```
radial-gradient(center center, ellipse cover, white, blue);
```

was changed to:

```
radial-gradient(cover ellipse at center center, white, blue);
```

Unfortunately, this new syntax is not well supported across browsers at the
time of writing this book. So we'll stick with the old syntax, which instead has
a good support.

Shadows

Shadows are implemented in CSS3 with two different properties sharing similar syntaxes, `box-shadow` and `text-shadow`. Let's create another example to showcase how they work:

```html
<!doctype html>
<html>
<head>
  <meta charset="utf8">
  <title>Explore Shadows!</title>

  <style>
    .box{
      width: 400px;
      height: 80px;
      border: 3px solid rgb(60,60,60);
      margin: 30px auto;
      border-radius: 5px;
      line-height: 80px;
      text-align: center;
    }
    #outset{
      box-shadow: 10px 10px 3px rgb(0,0,0);
    }
    #inset{
      box-shadow: 10px 10px 3px rgb(0,0,0) inset;
    }
    #offset{
      box-shadow: 0px 0px 0px 10px rgb(0,0,0);
    }
    #text{
      text-shadow: 10px 10px 3px rgb(0,0,0);
    }

  </style>

  <script src="js/prefixfree.js"></script>
</head>
<body>
  <section>

    <div id="outset" class="box"></div>
    <div id="inset" class="box"></div>
    <div id="offset" class="box"></div>
    <div id="text" class="box">Some text</div>

  </section>
</body>
</html>
```

Essentially, box-shadow and text-shadow are similar. Both of these properties have shadow offset (first two parameters) and blur (third parameter). Only box-shadow has the optional fourth parameter that controls the spread of the shadow or distance of blur.

Next comes the color, and then, optionally and only for the box-shadow property, an extra keyword, inset, that results in a shadow dropped inside the element and not outside. Finally, more shadows can be defined, separated by commas (,).

The following screenshot shows the result of the preceding code executed in a browser:

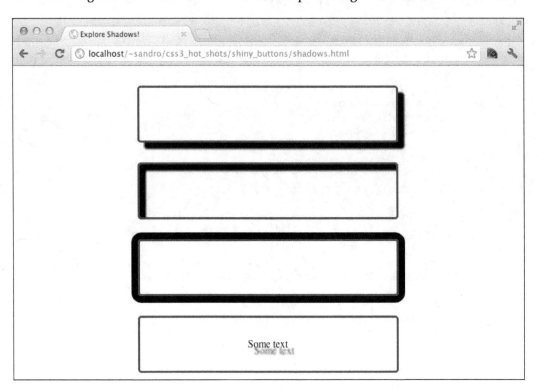

With this new knowledge, we can now add more effects to our push buttons. Let's add some more properties to application.css:

```css
/* shadows */
#arcade_game a:before{
  box-shadow:
    0px 0px 10px rgba(0,0,80,0.7),
    0px 0px 4px rgba(0,0,0,0.4), 3px 3px 6px rgba(0,0,0, 0.5),
    2px 2px 1px  rgba(255,255,255,0.3) inset,
    10px 10px 20px rgba(0,0,0,0.1) inset;
}
```

```
#arcade_game a:after{
  box-shadow:
    1px 0px 1px rgba(0,0,0, 0.7),
    6px 0px 4px rgba(0,0,0, 0.6),
    0px 1px 0px rgba(200,200,200,0.7) inset,
    2px 2px 1px  rgba(255,255,255,0.3) inset;
}
```

Then, reload the project in the browser.

Adding labels

Each button must have its own symbol on it. To obtain this result, we can use an HTML5 `data-*` attribute, such as `data-symbol`. HTML5 considers all `data-*` attributes valid and free for developers to be used to hold some application-specific information, such as in this case. We can then insert the value of the custom attribute inside the push button using the `content` property. Let's see how, but first we need to update our `<a>` elements. So let's edit `index.html`:

```
<a href="#" class="punch" data-symbol="!">PUNCH</a>
<a href="#" class="jump" data-symbol="★">JUMP</a>
```

 To type the Black star (★) (Unicode character: U+2605), we can do a copy and paste from http://www.fileformat.info/info/unicode/char/2605/index.htm, or we can use the character map included in Windows.

Next, we need to add proper instructions to `application.css`:

```css
/* text */
#arcade_game a:before{
  font-family: 'Chango', cursive;
  text-align: center;
  color: rgba(255,255,255, 0.4);
  text-shadow: -1px -1px 2px rgba(10,10,10, 0.3);
  content: attr(data-symbol);
}
```

The following screenshot shows the result in the browser:

Indeed, we can change the button's symbol simply by modifying the value of the `data-symbol` attribute.

Handling mouse clicks

Almost done! Now we need to make the button a bit more responsive. To achieve this, we can take advantage of the `:active` pseudo-selector to modify some shadows. Let's add the following lines to `application.css`:

```css
/* active */
#arcade_game a:active:before{
  background-image: none;
  box-shadow:
    0px 0px 7px rgba(0,0,80,0.7),
    0px 0px 4px rgba(0,0,0,0.4),
    10px 10px 20px rgba(0,0,0,0.3) inset;
```

```
    line-height: 65px;
}

#arcade_game a:active:after{
  background-image:
    -moz-radial-gradient(7px 7px, ellipse farthest-side,
    rgba(255,255,255,0.8), rgba(255,255,255,0.6) 3px,
    rgba(200,200,200,0.0) 20px),
    -moz-radial-gradient(53px 53px, rgba(255,255,255,0),
    rgba(255,255,255,0) 33px, rgba(255,255,255,0.3) 36px,
    rgba(255,255,255,0.3) 36px, rgba(255,255,255,0) 36px);
  background-image:
    radial-gradient(7px 7px, ellipse farthest-side,
    rgba(255,255,255,0.8), rgba(255,255,255,0.6) 3px,
    rgba(200,200,200,0.0) 20px),
    radial-gradient(53px 53px, rgba(255,255,255,0),
    rgba(255,255,255,0) 33px, rgba(255,255,255,0.3) 36px,
    rgba(255,255,255,0.3) 36px, rgba(255,255,255,0) 36px);
}
```

By increasing the value of the line-height property, we move the symbol down a bit, giving the illusion that it has been pushed down with the button. Let's reload the project in the browser and check the result:

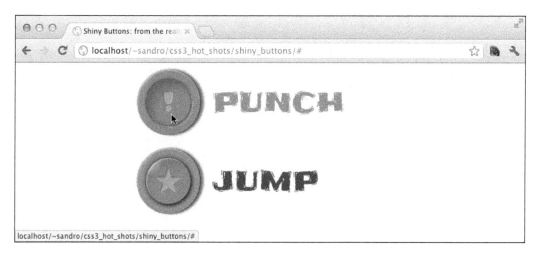

Small changes in CSS, big results

We have now completed the first kind of buttons. Before moving on to the next one, we better pause for a second to realize that all the shadows and gradients we have coded are basically colorless; they simply add white or black to the underlying color. This means that we can choose a different background color for each button. So let's add the following code to `application.css`:

```
/* puch */
#arcade_game .punch:after, #arcade_game .punch:before{
  background-color: rgb(123,26,55);
}

#arcade_game .punch{
  color: rgb(123,26,55);
}

/* jump */
#arcade_game .jump:after, #arcade_game .jump:before{
  background-color: rgb(107,140,86);
}

#arcade_game .jump{
  color:   rgb(107,140,86);
}
```

The following screenshot shows the result:

Creating an ON/OFF switch

Ok, now we'll style some checkbox buttons to try and match the appearance of some recording studio buttons ("REC"). The following is a screenshot of the final result:

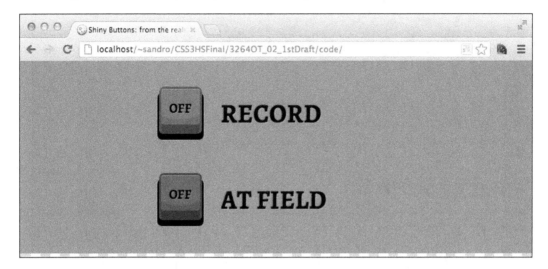

First, let's add the checkboxes to index.html, just after the previous article element:

```
<article id="old_panel">
  <form>
    <input type="checkbox" id="rec">
    <label class="rec" for="rec">RECORD</label>
    <input type="checkbox" id="at_field">
    <label class="at_field" for="at_field">AT FIELD</label>
  </form>
</article>
```

As we did in the previous chapter, we now want to hide the input element. Let's do this by adding a few lines to application.css:

```
#old_panel input{
  visibility: hidden;
  position: absolute;
  top: -999px;
  clip: 'rect(0,0,0,0)';
}

#old_panel label{
  display: block;
  position: relative;
```

```
   width: 300px;
   padding-left: 125px;
   cursor: pointer;
   line-height: 140px;
   height: 130px;
   font-family: 'Alegreya SC', serif;
   font-size: 40px;
   margin: 0px auto;
   text-shadow: 1px 1px 1px rgba(255,255,255, 0.3), -1px -1px 1px
rgba(10,10,10, 0.3);
}
```

Good! We want this element to act like some sort of button, so we force the cursor to assume the pointer icon by using the `cursor` property.

Creating a mask

Now we set a background color for the `article` element. This is fairly important for what we're going to build.

```
#old_panel{
   background: rgb(150,130,90);
   padding: 9px 0px 20px 0px;
}
```

Next, we focus on the `:before` and `:after` pseudo-selectors:

```
#old_panel label:before{
   content: '';
   z-index: 1;
   display: block;
   position: absolute;
   bottom: 0px;
   left: 0px;
   width: 126px;
   height: 131px;
   background-image:
     -moz-radial-gradient(50% 50%, circle,
     rgba(0,0,0,0.0),
     rgba(0,0,0,0.0) 50px,
     rgb(150,130,90) 50px);
   background-image:
     radial-gradient(50% 50%, circle,
     rgba(0,0,0,0.0),
     rgba(0,0,0,0.0) 50px,
     rgb(150,130,90) 50px);
}
```

What we've done now is to use a gradient as a sort of mask. In essence, we've created a transparent circle with a radius of 50px, and then we used the background color to cover the remaining area.

Ok, now the tricky part. To emulate the shape of the button, we create a box with rounded corners, and then we use the box-shadow property to give the illusion of height:

```
#old_panel label:after{
  content: 'OFF';
  display: block;
  position: absolute;
  font-size: 20px;
  text-align: center;
  line-height: 60px;
  z-index: 2;
  bottom: 30px;
  left: 30px;
  width: 60px;
  height: 65px;
  border-radius: 7px;
  background-image:
    -moz-radial-gradient(30px -15px, circle,
    rgba(255,255,255,0.1), rgba(255,255,255,0.1) 60px,
    rgba(255,255,255,0.0) 63px);
  background-image:
    radial-gradient(30px -15px, circle,
    rgba(255,255,255,0.1), rgba(255,255,255,0.1) 60px,
    rgba(255,255,255,0.0) 63px);
  box-shadow:
    0px 1px 0px rgba(255,255,255,0.3) inset,
    0px -11px 0px rgba(0,0,0,0.4) inset,
    -3px 9px 0px 0px black,
    3px 9px 0px 0px black,
    0px 10px 0px 0px rgba(255,255,255,0.3),
    -4px 9px 0px 0px rgba(255,255,255,0.3),
    4px 9px 0px 0px rgba(255,255,255,0.3),
    0px 0px 0px 30px rgb(150,130,90);

  border:
    3px solid rgba(0,0,0,0.2);
    border-bottom: 3px solid rgba(0,0,0,0.4);
  background-clip: padding-box;
}
```

The last of the shadow declared (the one highlighted) is also used as a mask. It has the same color as the background, and it spreads for 30px around the box we just created, covering the transparent area we declared with the previous gradient.

What is this all about? Let's try to explain it with a scheme:

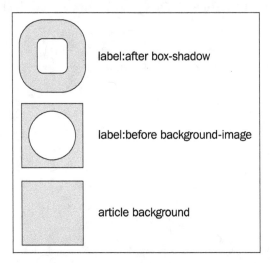

The preceding diagram displays the three shapes we used one above the other. If we turn off the box-shadow one, then every color set with the background-color property on label:before will be visible within the mask created by the background-image property of label:before.

To see what we've done so far, let's load the project in a browser:

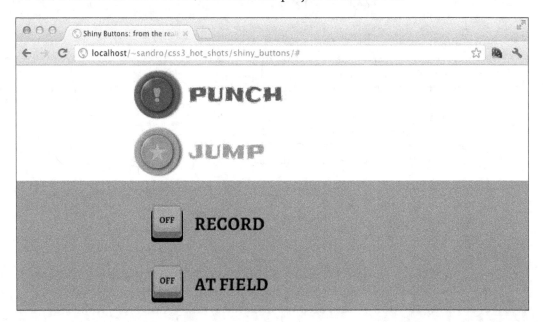

The active state

Now we need to handle the active state as we've done before. To simulate the pressure, we lower the height of the element and change the offset of some shadows.

```
#old_panel label:active:after{
  height: 54px;
  box-shadow:
    0px 0px 0px 3px black,
    -3px 9px 0px 0px black,
    3px 9px 0px 0px black,
    0px 0px 0px 4px rgba(255,255,255,0.3),
    0px 10px 0px 0px rgba(255,255,255,0.3),
    -4px 9px 0px 0px rgba(255,255,255,0.1),
    4px 9px 0px 0px rgba(255,255,255,0.1),
    0px 0px 0px 30px rgb(150,130,90);
}
```

Let's try this in the browser:

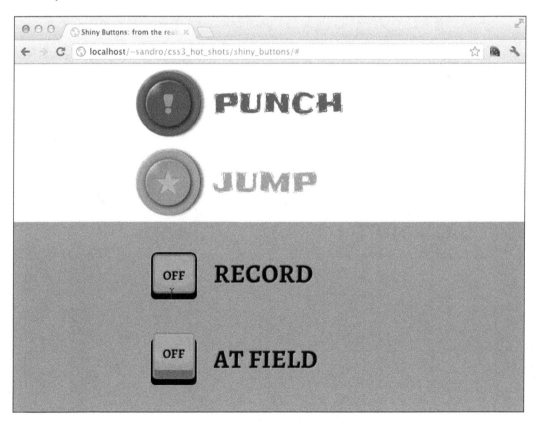

Adding the checked state

What we want to do now, basically, is to change the text of the label from OFF to ON and remove the box-shadow mask in order to expose a background color that we'll use to simulate a light propagating from the button.

```css
#old_panel input:checked + label:not(:active):after{
  content: 'ON';
  background-clip: border-box;
  box-shadow:
    0px 1px 0px rgba(255,255,255,0.3) inset,
    0px -11px 0px rgba(0,0,0,0.4) inset,
    -3px 9px 0px 0px black,
    3px 9px 0px 0px black,
    0px 10px 0px 0px rgba(255,255,255,0.3),
    -4px 9px 0px 0px rgba(255,255,255,0.3),
    4px 9px 0px 0px rgba(255,255,255,0.3);
}

#old_panel input:checked + label:not(:active):before{
  background-image:
    -moz-radial-gradient(50% 57%, circle,
    rgba(150,130,90,0.0),
    rgba(150,130,90,0.3) 40px,
    rgb(150,130,90) 55px);
  background-image:
    radial-gradient(50% 57%, circle, rgba(150,130,90,0.0),
    rgba(150,130,90,0.3) 40px,
    rgb(150,130,90) 55px);
}
```

We don't want to activate this effect while the button is still pressed, so we have added the :not(:active) pseudo-selector.

Adding colors

Let's set different colors for each button. This time, we need to specify one color for the OFF state and one for the ON state:

```css
/* -- record -- */
#old_panel input:checked + label.rec:not(:active):before, #old_panel
input:checked + label.rec:not(:active):after{
  background-color: rgb(248,36,21);
}

#old_panel label.rec:before{
  background-color: rgb(145,67,62);
}
```

```
/* -- at field -- */
#old_panel input:checked + label.at_field:not(:active):before, #old_
panel input:checked + label.at_field:not(:active):after{
  background-color: rgb(61,218,216);
}

#old_panel label.at_field:before{
  background-color: rgb(29,51,200);
}
```

And the following screenshot shows the result:

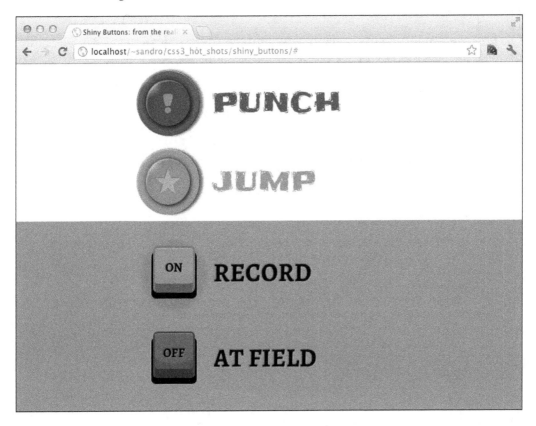

Supporting older browsers

This project is not meant to degrade gracefully on older browsers, so we need to apply a different technique to detect when features essential to this project are missing and provide an alternative CSS2 stylesheet.

For this, we rely on a JavaScript library called `Modernizr.js` (http://modernizr.com/), which shows methods for each HTML5/CSS3 feature. These methods simply return `true` or `false` depending on the presence of the desired feature. Then, we are going to use a small library included in `Modernizr.js`, called yepnope.js, (http://yepnopejs.com) to dynamically choose which stylesheet we want to load.

First of all, we need to download the library. To do so, we have to mark the checkboxes corresponding to which features we want to test, from the download page at http://modernizr.com/download/. Let's mark **border-radius**, **box-shadow**, **CSS Gradients**, and **multiple backgrounds**. Then, hit the **Generate** button, and then the **Download** button, saving the file as `modernizr.js` under the `js` folder for our project.

Ok, now we need to change something within the `<head>` tag of our `index.html` file to make this new trick work. The new `<head>` section is shown as follows:

```
<head>
  <meta charset="utf8">
  <meta http-equiv="X-UA-Compatible" content="IE=edge" />
  <title>Shiny Buttons: from the reality to the web!</title>
  <link
href='http://fonts.googleapis.com/css?family=Chango|Frijole|Alegre
ya+SC:700' rel='stylesheet' type='text/css'>
  <link rel="stylesheet" type="text/css"
href="http://yui.yahooapis.com/3.4.1/build/cssreset/cssreset-
min.css">
  <script
src="http://html5shiv.googlecode.com/svn/trunk/html5.js"></script>
  <script src="js/modernizr.js"></script>
  <script>
    yepnope({
      test : Modernizr.borderradius && Modernizr.boxshadow &&
Modernizr.multiplebgs && Modernizr.cssgradients,
      yep  : ['css/application.css','js/prefixfree.js'],
      nope : 'css/olderbrowsers.css'
    });
  </script>

</head>
```

We've just got to remember to create a `css/olderbrowsers.css` file containing some CSS2 instructions to style these elements for older browsers, such as the following instructions:

```
#arcade_game a{
  display: block;
  margin: 20px auto;
  width: 200px;
  text-align: center;
```

```
  font-family: 'Frijole', cursive;
  font-size: 40px;
  color: white;
  text-decoration: none;
}

/* puch */
#arcade_game .punch{
  background-color: rgb(123,26,55);
}

/* jump */
#arcade_game .jump{
  background-color: rgb(107,140,86);
}

#old_panel{
  text-align: center;
}

#old_panel label{
  font-family: 'Alegreya SC', serif;
  font-size: 40px;
}
```

We also have to consider that relying only on JavaScript may sometimes be a hazardous choice because we aren't providing a non-JavaScript alternative. An easy workaround might be setting olderbrowsers.css as the default stylesheet and then dynamically loading application.css only when the required CSS3 properties are supported.

To do so, however, we have to add a few lines to application.css to void the olderbrowsers.css properties:

```
/* === [BEGIN] VOIDING BASE CSS2 === */

#arcade_game a{
  background-color: transparent !important;
  width: 300px !important;
  text-align: left !important;
}

#old_panel{
  text-align: left !important;
}

/* === [END] VOIDING BASE CSS2 === */
```

Finally, we can change our previous HTML code as follows:

```
<link rel="stylesheet" type="text/css"
href="css/olderbrowsers.css">
<script>
  yepnope({
    test : Modernizr.borderradius && Modernizr.boxshadow &&
Modernizr.multiplebgs && Modernizr.cssgradients,
    yep  : ['css/application.css','js/prefixfree.js']
  });
</script>
```

Supporting IE10

Internet Explorer 10 supports all the CSS features shows in this project. However, we have to face the fact that Prefix Free doesn't add the `-ms-` experimental prefix on the `radial-gradient` notation. This is not a big problem because our buttons works well without gradients too, except for the `radial-gradient` notation we used as a mask in the ON/OFF switch. To find a way around this, we can add the following lines to `application.css`:

```
#old_panel label:before{
  background-image:
  -ms-radial-gradient(50% 50%, circle,
  rgba(0,0,0,0.0),
  rgba(0,0,0,0.0) 50px,
  rgb(150,130,90) 50px);
}
```

Summary

This project goes into details with gradients and shadows, demonstrating how these properties can be employed to achieve amazing effects using a very small set of HTML elements.

Before moving on to the next chapter, it might be useful to know that there are a few online gradient generators that let us compose a gradient using a nice UI and then provide us the right CSS syntax to include in our stylesheet. They can be found at `http://www.colorzilla.com/gradient-editor/`, `http://www.cssbuttongenerator.com/`, and `http://css3generator.com/`.

In the next chapter, we'll learn how to deal with multiple device visualizations by creating a menu that works on both desktop and smartphones!

3
Omni Menu

With media queries, we can activate or deactivate CSS instructions when some device or viewport requirements are met. This is especially useful when we have to deal with elements that need to have different representations depending on the user's device. The menu is usually such an element. In this chapter we will develop a main menu system that displays perfectly on desktop browsers and mobile devices; we can call it Omni Menu. We're going to cover the following topics:

- Setup operations
- First level
- Second level
- Moving parts
- Basic transitions
- Introducing animations
- Adding some colors
- Media queries
- Mobile version
- Improving speed

In the next section we'll start creating a basic HTML menu structure. As usual, we can store all of the project's files in a folder named as the name of the project (`omni_menu` in this case). Before we begin, let's look at a screenshot of the final result:

Setup operations

To style the menu, we need to define the markup first. Let's write a small HTML file, `index.html`, where we will define a classic two-level menu structure using `li` and `ul` items. Next, we'll add some basic CSS before moving to the central part of the chapter.

```html
<!doctype html>
<html>
<head>
  <meta charset="utf-8">
  <meta http-equiv="X-UA-Compatible" content="IE=edge" />

  <title> Omnimenu: good for desktop, good for mobile </title>

  <link rel="stylesheet" type="text/css"
href="http://yui.yahooapis.com/3.7.3/build/cssreset/
cssreset-min.css" data-noprefix>

  <link rel="stylesheet" type="text/css"
href="css/application.css">

  <script src="js/prefixfree.js"></script>
</head>
<body>
```

```
<nav>
  <ul>
    <li data-section="about-me">
      <a href="#" class="item"> About me </a>
      <ul>
        <li><a href="#" class="item">Early years</a></li>
        <li><a href="#" class="item">First works</a></li>
        <li><a href="#" class="item">Today and tomorrow</a></li>
        <li class="cursor"><a href="#" class="item"> back </a>
        </li>
      </ul>
    </li>
    <li data-section="portfolio">
      <a href="#" class="item"> Portfolio </a>
      <ul>
        <li> <a href="#" class="item"> Design </a> </li>
        <li> <a href="#" class="item"> Articles </a> </li>
        <li class="cursor"> <a href="#" class="item"> back </a>
        </li>
      </ul>
    </li>
    <li data-section="interests">
      <a href="#" class="item"> Interests </a>
      <ul>
        <li> <a href="#" class="item"> Skying </a> </li>
        <li> <a href="#" class="item"> Snowboarding </a> </li>
        <li> <a href="#" class="item"> Wakeboarding </a> </li>
        <li class="cursor"> <a href="#" class="item"> back </a>
        </li>
      </ul>
    </li>
    <li class="cursor"></li>
  </ul>
</nav>

</body>
</html>
```

We take advantage of the new data-* attributes to enhance semantically the items in the first level of our menu. We'll also see in a moment how these attributes can help us better style this structure.

Now let's open `application.css` and define a basic CSS structure to center this menu and add a nice background. For this part of the project we don't focus on a mobile layout, so we can use a classic 960 px approach:

```css
/* === [BEGIN] Style === */
html{
   height: 100%;
}

body{
   background-image: repeating-linear-gradient(315deg, #ddd, #ddd
40px, #aaa 40px, #aaa 80px);
   padding: 20px;
   height: 100%;
}

nav{
   margin: 0 auto;
   width: 960px;
   font-family: sans-serif;
   font-size: 0.6em;
   background-color: rgb(86,86,86);
   background-image: linear-gradient(bottom, rgb(75,75,75),
rgb(86,86,86));
   border-radius: 4px;
   box-shadow: 0 0 10px rgba(0,0,0,0.1), 0 -1.5em 0 rgba(0,0,0,0.1)
inset, 0 1px 1px 1px rgba(0,0,0,0.1) inset;
}

nav > ul{
   padding: 0 10px;
}

/* === [END] Style === */
```

The highlighted part in the previous code defines a collapsed gradient in order to obtain a striped background. Next we define the size of the nav element to 960px and put some nice gradient, shadows, and a border radius on it.

If we load the project in a CSS3 compatible browser, we can view the effects of our first styling:

Styling the first-level items

The typical format in many two-level menus is to display the first-level items horizontally on the same line and then hide the second-level ones. We will add some CSS code to `application.css` to accomplish this, as follows:

```
nav > ul > li{
  display: inline-block;
  vertical-align: top;
  line-height: 3em;
  width: 100px;
  z-index: 2;
  position: relative;
  border-left: 1px solid #313131;
  box-shadow: 1px 0 1px rgba(255,255,255,0.1) inset, -1px 0 1px
rgba(255,255,255,0.1) inset;
}

nav > ul > li:nth-last-child(2){
  border-right: 1px solid #313131;
}

nav > ul > li > ul{
  position: absolute;
  left: -1px;
  top: 3em;
  clip: rect(0,0,0,0);
  opacity: 0;
}
```

Using the inline-block display

In the previous code, we used `display: inline-block` instead of floating the elements as is commonly done. Both these properties are commonly used to align elements inline, but the difference is that `display: inline-block` doesn't break the page flow and saves us from using `clearfix`. However, there's a drawback to using the `display: inline-block` property. Let's see it in a small demo:

```html
<!doctype html>
<html>
  <head>
    <title>inline-block demo</title>
    <style>
      div{
        display: inline-block;
        width: 100px;
        border: 1px solid black;
        height: 30px;
        line-height: 30px;
        text-align: center;
      }
    </style>
  </head>
  <body>
    <div> ONE </div>
    <div> TWO </div>
    <div> THREE </div><div> FOUR </div>
  </body>
</html>
```

If we load our demo page in a browser, the result is as follows:

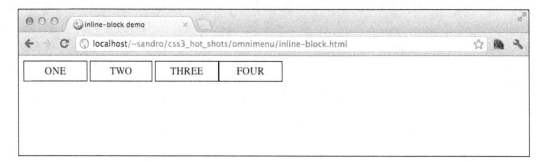

You will notice that there is no space between **THREE** and **FOUR** but there are spaces between **ONE**, **TWO**, and **THREE**. Why is that so? This is because `display: inline-block` takes into account the spaces between the elements in the HTML markup. To avoid this issue, we will take care to ensure that we have consistent space or line breaks between each element.

Using new pseudo-selectors

Now, let's move to the next interesting instruction: `nth-last-child(2)`. This is one of the many new pseudo-selectors introduced by CSS3. With `nth-last-child(n)` we can target the `nth` element counting from the last, and with `nth-child(n)` we can do the same but starting from the top. These two pseudo-selectors can also be used to select elements through some kind of pattern. For example, suppose we want to highlight only the even elements of the following list:

```
<ul>
  <li>1</li>
  <li>2</li>
  <li>3</li>
  <li>4</li>
  <li>5</li>
  <li>6</li>
</ul>
```

We can achieve this with the following simple CSS code:

```
li:nth-child(2n){
  background: yellow;
}
```

If instead we want to target only the elements with index greater than three, we can use the following CSS:

```
li:nth-child(n+4){
  background: yellow;
}
```

The following screenshot shows the result of the previous example:

Completing the first level

We still have to add a few CSS properties to complete the styling of our first-level elements:

```
nav .item{
  color: #fff;
  text-shadow: 1px 1px 0 rgba(0,0,0,0.5);
  text-decoration: none;
  font-weight: bold;
  text-transform: uppercase;
  letter-spacing: 0.2em;
  padding-left: 10px;
  white-space: nowrap;
  display: block;
  cursor: pointer;
}
```

Well done! Now let's run the project in a CSS3-compatible browser to appreciate the results:

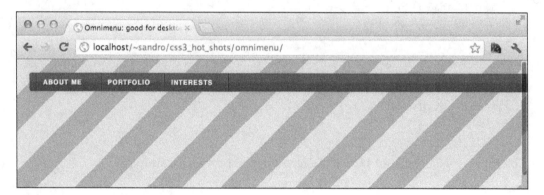

Styling submenus

Now we have to style the second-level items. Well, to be honest, we have already hidden them in the previous section in order to obtain a nice first-level styling, but now we can enrich the second-level elements with plenty of more properties and make sure they show up when users hover the mouse on their first-level parent.

Let's start with the last part we just discussed. In order to display the second-level elements, we have to use the :hover pseudo-selector:

```
nav > ul > li > .item:hover + ul,
nav > ul > li > ul:hover{
   clip: auto;
   /* temporary property, to be removed */
   opacity: 1;
}
```

We have intercepted both the hover on the parent and on all of the children in order to keep the second-level menu displayed even when the mouse moves on them. Once done, we can start with some basic styling:

```
nav > ul > li > ul{
   padding: 0.7em 0px;
   border-bottom-left-radius: 5px;
   border-bottom-right-radius: 5px;
   border-top: none;
   background-color: rgb(117,189,70);
   background-color: rgba(119,172,48, 0.8);
   background-image: linear-gradient(left, rgba(117,189,70,1),
rgba(117,189,70, 0.0));
}

nav > ul > li > ul > li > .item{
   text-align: left;
   min-width: 100px;
   padding: 0px 10px;
   line-height: 2.5em;
}

nav > ul > li > ul > li{
   display: block;
   position: relative;
   z-index: 4;
}
```

There is just one small thing to underline here. Within the highlighted part of the previous code, there is an easy and simple fallback mechanism for browsers that do not support CSS3. If we first declare an rgb background-color value and then an rgba one, we ensure that browsers that do not support CSS3 apply the rgb instruction and skip the rgba one, whereas browsers that do support CSS3 overwrite the rgb instruction with the rgba one.

Ok, time to reload the project in our preferred CSS3 browser and test the results:

In the next section, we're going to add some basic CSS in order to respond to mouse movements. For example, activating a particular submenu when the mouse is placed over its parent first-level menu.

Moving parts

We have added a (yet unused) `<li class="cursor">` element at the end of the first and second levels. What we want to create is a block that is able to move under the element when the mouse hovers over it. It's a nice effect, and to achieve it we are going to use CSS3 transitions. But first let's create the same effect without animation:

```css
nav > ul{
    position: relative;
}

nav li.cursor{
    position: absolute;
    background-color: #75BD46;
    text-indent: 900px;
    border: none;
    height: 3em;
    z-index: 1;
    left: 11px;
    clip: rect(0,0,0,0);
    box-shadow:
        0px 0px 10px rgba(0,0,0,0.1),
        0px -1.5em 0px rgba(0,0,0,0.1) inset,
        0px 1px 1px 1px rgba(0,0,0,0.1) inset;
}
```

```
nav li.cursor a{
  display: none;
}

nav > ul > li > ul > li.cursor{
  height: 2.5em;
  left: 0px;
  width: 100%;
  bottom: 0.7em;
  box-shadow: none;
  background-image: none;
  background-color: rgb(165,204,60);
  background-color: rgba(165,204,60,0.7);
  z-index: 3;
}

nav > ul li:hover ~ li.cursor{
  clip: auto;
}

nav > ul > li:hover + li + li + li.cursor{
  left: 11px;
}

nav > ul > li:hover + li + li.cursor{
  left: 112px;
}

nav > ul > li:hover + li.cursor{
  left: 213px;
}

nav > ul > li > ul > li:hover + li + li + li.cursor{
  bottom: 5.7em;
}

nav > ul > li > ul > li:hover + li + li.cursor{
  bottom: 3.2em;
}

nav > ul > li > ul > li:hover + li.cursor{
  bottom: 0.7em;
}

nav li.cursor .item{
  display: none;
}
```

The highlighted code shows the special selector we use to toggle the visibility of our .cursor element. Basically, we display it if one of the previous li elements are hovered by the mouse.

Next, we have to define the absolute position of the .cursor element, which obviously depends on the li element we're hovering. To achieve this behavior, we chain the + selector in order to precisely move the cursor under the element. The same is done for the second-level elements.

If we run the project in our browser, we may experience some disappointment. The effect is exactly the same as simply changing the li background using the :hover pseudo-selector.

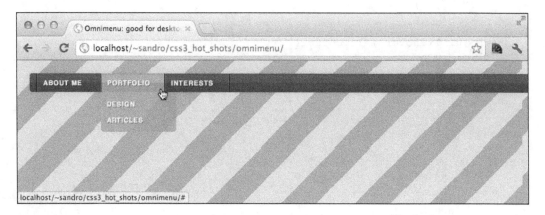

Ok, time to add our hidden ingredient: transitions.

Adding transitions

The logic behind transitions is simple yet powerful. We can instruct the browser to create an animation between two different property values. That's it! We can use the transition property to specify that when a change occurs in another CSS property (for example, width), the element should not switch from one value to the other instantaneously but take a desired amount of time, thus creating an animation between the two values. The following example illustrates this effect:

```
<!doctype html>
<html>
  <head>
    <title>basic animation</title>
    <style>
      a{
        display: block;
```

```
        width: 300px;
        line-height: 100px;
        height: 100px;
        text-align: center;
        font-size: 50px;
        font-family: sans-serif;
        font-weight: bold;
        color: black;
        border: 10px solid black;
        text-decoration: none;
        transition: all 1s;
        -ms-transition: all 1s;
      }
      a:hover{
        color: red;
      }
    </style>
    <script src="js/prefixfree.js"></script>
  </head>
  <body>
    <a href="#"> HOVER ME </a>
  </body>
</html>
```

The `all` keyword tells the browser to take exactly one second to change from one property to the other for all the properties that support transition. In this case, when we hover the a element, the `color` property changes from `black` to `red`, but not instantaneously; instead, it covers all the colors between black and red in one second with a really cool effect.

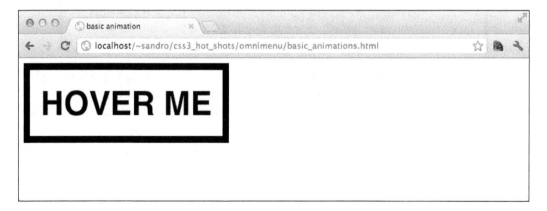

We can do this trick with a lot of other properties and in many other ways, as we'll see in the later chapters of this book. For the moment, we can use what we have learned to enhance our project. Let's add a `transition` statement to `application.css`:

```
nav li.cursor{
  -ms-transition: all 1s;
  transition: all 1s;
}
```

With this simple property, we have obtained a whole new result. Now every time we hover an element, the cursor moves under that element in a really smooth animation.

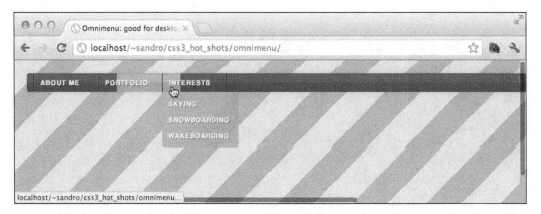

At the time of writing this book, `prefixfree.js` did not support transitions and animations in Internet Explorer 10. So we have to remember to add a copy of the transition property with the `-ms-` experimental prefix. This is likely to change in the future, both because Microsoft will remove the need of experimental vendor prefixes, and because of a new version of this JavaScript library.

Now we have to handle another problem. The second-level menu appears too soon, with an unpleasant effect. How can we delay its appearance until the `.cursor` element has reached the right position under the `li` element? We will see this in the next section.

Introducing animations

Animations are one-step-forward transitions. With them, we can control the transition between one or more properties in detail. An animation is composed of a set of keyframes where each keyframe is basically a way to declare which values our chosen properties must have at a specific progress percentage of the animation. Let's explore this feature with the following example:

```
<!doctype html>
<html>
  <head>
    <title>basic animation</title>
    <style>
      div{
        position: absolute;
        top: 0px;
        left: 0px;
        width: 100px;
        height: 100px;
        border: 10px solid black;
        background-color: red;
        text-decoration: none;
        -ms-animation: fouredges 5s linear 2s infinite alternate;
        animation: fouredges 5s linear 2s infinite alternate;
      }

      @-ms-keyframes fouredges{
        0%   { top: 0px; left: 0px;}
        25%  { top: 0px; left: 100px;}
        50%  { top: 100px; left: 100px;}
        75%  { top: 100px; left: 0px;}
        100% { top: 0px; left: 0px;}
      }

      @keyframes fouredges{
        0%   { top: 0px; left: 0px;}
        25%  { top: 0px; left: 100px;}
        50%  { top: 100px; left: 100px;}
        75%  { top: 100px; left: 0px;}
        100% { top: 0px; left: 0px;}
      }

    </style>
    <script src="js/prefixfree.js"></script>
  </head>
  <body>
    <div></div>
  </body>
</html>
```

With the @keyframes statement, we define the value of some properties of our choice during a progression from 0% to 100%. Once this is done, we can use the animation property with a few parameters, defined as follows:

- First parameter: It specifies the name of the animation we want to execute on the element (for example, fouredges in the previous code).

- Second parameter: It specifies the total amount of time we want a single loop through the animation to take place in.

- Third parameter: It specifies the accelerating function. Basically, we can decide whether the element should move at a constant velocity (with the keyword linear) or accelerate during the beginning or ending phase of each step of the animation (using ease-in, ease-out, or ease).

- Fourth parameter: It specifies the delay we want to apply to the beginning of the animation.

- Fifth parameter: It specifies the number of times we want the animation to be repeated. infinite is a valid value for this parameter as well as positive numbers.

- Sixth parameter: With the keyword alternate, we can ask the browser to toggle the direction of the animation. In other words, the animation will go first from 0% to 100%, and then from 100% to 0%, and over again.

If we try the example we just wrote in a browser, we'll see a square moving along a four-vertex path:

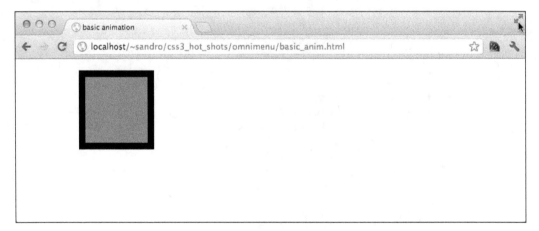

Well, that sounds interesting, but how can this help us with our project? Simple! We can use a delayed animation (an animation with some delay) to create a fade-in effect in the second-level menus. So let's remove the `opacity: 1` temporary property we added earlier and add some CSS to `application.css`:

```
nav > ul > li > .item:hover + ul,
nav > ul > li > ul:hover{
   animation: fadein 0.1s linear 0.9s;
   -ms-animation: fadein 0.1s linear 0.9s;
   animation-fill-mode: forwards;
   -ms-animation-fill-mode: forwards;
}

@keyframes fadein{
   1% {
      opacity: 0.0;
   }

   100% {
      opacity: 1.0;
   }
}

@-ms-keyframes fadein{
   1% {
      opacity: 0.0;
   }

   100% {
      opacity: 1.0;
   }
}
```

The `animation-fill-mode: forwards` property tells the browser not to revert to `0%` at the end of the animation, but to keep the `100%` position.

With these new add-ons in our project, we can now try an almost complete desktop version in our browser. Enjoy the cursor animation and the second-level menu's fade-in effect.

With the previous lines of code we have, however, removed the support to browsers that don't handle CSS3 animations, in particular for IE9 and below. To handle this problem there are a lot of techniques, most of which will be unveiled during the course of this book. The first technique that we'll implement works by substituting the <html> tag with something slightly more complex, as follows:

```
<!--[if lte IE 9]> <html class="lteie9"> <![endif]-->
<!--[if !IE]> --> <html> <!-- <![endif]-->
```

By using conditional comments, we can now identify when the user is browsing our website using IE9 or less because a new .lteie9 class gets added to the html element.

So we can add a small chunk of code to our CSS file that gets triggered only when .lteie9 is present:

```
.lteie9 nav > ul > li > .item:hover + ul,
.lteie9 nav > ul > li > ul:hover{
  opacity: 1;
}
```

Adding colors

We can easily change the color of the .cursor element depending on which element the mouse is hovering. We'll also observe how the colors will change gradually, thanks to our transition: all 1s property, thus creating a really nice effect.

Let's add some properties to application.css to change the color of the .cursor element, and to add some colors to the second-level menus:

```
/* portfolio */
li[data-section=portfolio]:hover ~ li.cursor {
  background-color: #468DBD;
}

nav > ul > li[data-section=portfolio] > ul{
  background-color: rgb(70, 141, 189);
  background-color: rgba(60, 194, 204, 0.8);
  background-image: linear-gradient(left, rgba(70, 141, 189,1),
rgba(70, 141, 189, 0.0));
}
```

```
nav > ul > li[data-section=portfolio] > ul > li.cursor{
  background-color: rgb(60, 194, 204);
  background-color: rgba(60, 194, 204, 0.7);
}

/* interests */
li[data-section=interests]:hover ~ li.cursor {
  background-color: #9E5CD0;
}

nav > ul > li[data-section=interests] > ul{
  background-color: rgb(158, 92, 208);
  background-color: rgba(186, 99, 195, 0.8);
  background-image: linear-gradient(left, rgba(158, 92, 208, 1),
rgba(158, 92, 208, 0.0));
}

nav > ul > li[data-section=interests] > ul > li.cursor{
  background-color: rgb(186, 99, 195);
  background-color: rgba(186, 99, 195, 0.7);
}
```

In the previous code, we target three different elements. First the `.cursor` element when the `li` element with attribute `data-section-portfolio` is in state `:hover`, next the second-level menu corresponding to the `li` element with attribute `data-section-portfolio`, and finally the `.cursor` element for this second-level menu. In this case, it is particularly useful to take advantage of a `data-*` attribute to mark semantically each item of the menu.

Let's reload the project in the browser to view and experience the effect:

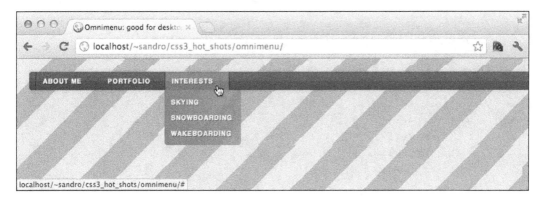

Media queries

Media queries is a simple yet incredibly powerful tool to activate some CSS properties, depending on certain browser and device characteristics, such as the browser's viewport size, the device's width and height, and orientation. Before diving into the details, let's write a small script to experiment with this feature:

```html
<!doctype html>
<html>
  <head>
    <title>media queries</title>
    <style>
    ul{
      margin: 0;
      padding: 0;
    }
    li{
      list-style-type: none;
      border: 2px solid black;
      margin: 5px;
      padding: 0px 10px;
      display: inline-block;
    }

    @media screen and (max-width: 400px){
      li{
        line-height: 20px;
        text-align: center;
        display: block;
      }

    }
    </style>
  </head>
  <body>
    <ul>
      <li>one</li>
      <li>two</li>
      <li>three</li>
      <li>four</li>
      <li>five</li>
      <li>six</li>
      <li>seven</li>
      <li>eight</li>
```

```
            <li>nine</li>
            <li>ten</li>
            <li>eleven</li>
            <li>twelve</li>
        </ul>
    </body>
</html>
```

In this example, we instruct the browser to apply the properties enclosed between the `@media` curly brackets *only* when the conditions expressed are satisfied. Let's have a look at them:

- `screen`: This keyword is one of the available media types, and is used to indicate which kind of media must implement the enclosed statements. There are plenty of media types described in the dedicated W3C specification (`http://www.w3.org/TR/CSS2/media.html#media-types`), but only a few of them (`screen`, `print`, `projection`) are actually supported by today's browsers.

- `max-width`: This is one of the many conditional keywords we can chain to list the characteristics that must be present in a device in order to activate the enclosing statements. The `max-width` keyword can be read as "up to", so this condition is verified until the browser's viewport size exceeds the given value.

If we run the previous code in a CSS3-compatible browser, we can see something like the following screenshot:

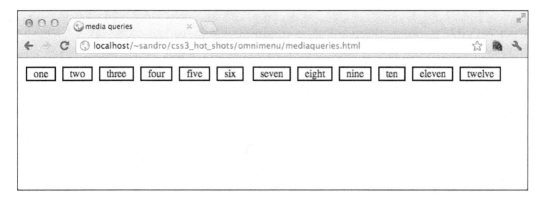

But if we adjust the size of the window below `400px`, the statements within the media query get activated and the result will be something like the following screenshot:

Cool, isn't it? Of course, there are other conditional keywords besides `max-width`. Let's have a look at them:

- `min-width`: This keyword can be read as "the viewport width is minimum x", where x is the value assigned to the `min-width` property.

- `max-height` and `min-height`: These keywords work in the same way as the `*-width` ones, but they are applied to the browser's viewport height.

- `min-device-width`, `max-device-width`, `min-device-height`, and `max-device-height`: These keywords identify the real dimensions of the device; so if we want to target only screens bigger than 1900 x 1200, we have to write a rule such as `(min-device-width: 1900px)` and `(min-device-height: 1200px)`.

- `orientation`: The value for this property can be either `portrait` or `landscape`. It identifies the current orientation of the device.

There are even more of such conditional keywords, but those not present in the previous list aren't so useful, and furthermore are not yet supported by any browser. Anyway, the full list can be viewed at http://www.w3.org/TR/css3-mediaqueries/#media1.

We can also define a media query in a `<link>` declaration using the `media` attribute, as follows:

```
<link rel="stylesheet" type="text/css" media="screen and
(max-device-width: 480px)" href="css/small.css" />
```

In this case, we have to take into account browsers that don't understand media query statements because they will always load the linked CSS regardless of the conditions. To prevent this behavior, at least on older versions of Internet Explorer, we can wrap the `<link>` element with a conditional comment:

```
<!-- [if gte IE 9]> -->
<link rel="stylesheet" type="text/css" media="screen and
(max-width: 480px)" href="css/small.css" />
<!-- <![endif]-->
```

Ok, now we know how media queries work, but how can we use this feature to target mobile devices? We can do it in two ways, using `max-device-width` or `max-width`.

The `max-device-width` property checks the size of the device, which makes it difficult to emulate on a desktop web browser or laptop. The other drawback of using this property is that we don't want to change our layout based on the size of the screen; we want to change it in response to the size of the browser window. Therefore, the preferred property is `max-width`, which is the behavior that will give us the most flexibility for our menu system.

Now that we have chosen the behavior to target mobile devices, we have another complication to resolve. In order to represent a desktop version of the page and then let the user zoom in and out, mobile devices fake their actual resolution. To force mobile browsers to expose their true dimensions and disable zoom, we can use a `<meta>` tag. This tag basically says that the maximum and minimum zoom factor must be equal to 1. Add the following line to `index.html`, just after the `<head>` tag:

```
<meta name="viewport" content="width=device-width,
initial-scale=1, maximum-scale=1">
```

Well done! Now all we have to do is find the size we want to use as a trigger to enable our "mobile" CSS. We'll use 320px, which is the size of an iPhone handled in portrait mode. So let's create a new `application_mobile.css` file under the `css` folder, and add the following `link` element just below the previous one in our `index.html` file:

```
<!-- [if gte IE 9]> -->
<link rel="stylesheet" type="text/css" media="screen and
(max-width: 320px)" href="css/application_mobile.css"/>
<!-- <![endif]-->
```

Styling the mobile version

Now we are ready to start styling the mobile version of this project. To accomplish this, we're going to transform the menu from a horizontal shape to a vertical one. Instead of having a second-level menu, we will instead create some cards and make them slide in when the corresponding first-level menu item is clicked.

So, first of all, let's write the necessary CSS to change the shape of our menu (within `application_mobile.css`):

```
nav {
    width: 290px;
    height: 100%;
    font-size: 1em;
    text-align: center;
    border-radius: 0;
    box-shadow: 0 0 5px rgba(0,0,0,0.4);
    position: relative;
    overflow: hidden;
}

nav > ul{
    width: 290px;
    padding: 0;
    position: absolute;
    top: 0;
    left: 0;
    z-index: 1;
}

nav > ul > li{
    width: 100%;
    display: block;
```

```
      position: static;
      border-bottom: 1px solid #313131;
      box-shadow:
         0 1px 1px rgba(255,255,255,0.1) inset,
         0 -1px 1px rgba(255,255,255,0.1) inset,
         0 -1.5em 0 rgba(0,0,0,0.1) inset;
}

nav > ul > li > .item {
      padding-right: 15px;
      position: relative;
      box-sizing: border-box;
      z-index: 1;
}

nav > ul > li > ul {
      display: block;
      padding: 0;
      padding-top: 3em;
      top: 0;
      left: 290px;
      height: 610px;
      width: 290px;
      clip: auto;
      opacity: 1;
      transition: left 1s;
      z-index: 2;
}
```

The first highlighted instruction shows how we can take advantage of a really useful property called box-sizing, which basically says which parts of an element are influenced when setting its width. The options are as follows:

- content-box: In this option, width refers only to the box that surrounds the element's content. Padding, margin, and border widths are excluded.

- padding-box: This option is the same as the previous one, but this time width includes padding. Border and margin widths are still excluded.

- border-box: This option is the same as the previous two, but this time only the margin width is excluded.

So when we write the following, we ask the browser to take care of 30 px of padding within the 100% width:

```
box-sizing: border-box;
width: 100%;
padding: 0px 15px;
```

If we now try to load the project in a mobile browser (for example, from the iPhone simulator), or if we resize our desktop browser window below 320 px, we can experiment with this layout:

We've already added the property transition: left 1s in the mobile version of the CSS code (application_mobile.css), so all we need to do is move the second-level menu to left: 0px when the corresponding first-level menu is clicked, in order to make it overlap the first-level menu. To achieve this, we can take advantage of the :hover pseudo-selector, which, in a mobile environment, is triggered when the user touches an element. So we can write the following:

```
nav > ul > li > .item:hover + ul{
    left: 0px;
```

```
    animation: none;
}

nav li.cursor{
  display:none;
  transition: none;
}

nav > ul > li > ul > li.cursor{
  display: block;
  top: 0px;
  text-indent: 0;
  left: 0px;
  line-height: 3em;
  height: 3em;
  clip: auto;
}

nav > ul > li > ul > li.cursor .item{
  display: block;
}

nav > ul > li > ul > li:first-child{
  border-top: 1px solid rgba(0,0,0,0.1);
}

nav > ul > li > ul > li{
  height: 3em;
  border-bottom: 1px solid rgba(0,0,0,0.1);
}

nav > ul > li > ul > li > .item{
  line-height: 3em;
  text-align: center;
}
```

The most important statement is the one highlighted; the others are there only to adjust some minor visual details. Now we can reload the project to appreciate the effects of the code we just wrote:

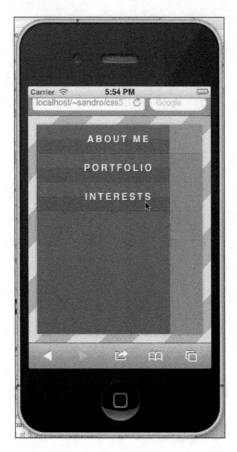

Handling the new layout on desktop browsers

What we did in the last chunk of code works on mobile devices, but fails on desktop browsers because of the difference in the behavior of the :hover pseudo-selector. Even though it is really unlikely that someone would ever explore this project from a desktop computer with a browser whose width is less than 320 px, we can use a bit of JavaScript to address this problem. The following is the code to add to index. html before the </head> tag:

```
<script
src="http://ajax.googleapis.com/ajax/libs/jquery/1.7.2/jquery.min.
js"></script>
<script
```

```
      src="http://cdnjs.cloudflare.com/ajax/libs/modernizr/2.5.3/
      modernizr.min.js"></script>
    <script>
      $(document).ready(function(){
      if(!Modernizr.touch){
        $('ul > li > .item').on('click', function(ev){
          $('ul > li').attr('data-status',null);
          $(ev.target).parent().attr('data-status','selected');
        });
        $('ul > li > ul > li > .item').on('click', function(ev){
          $(ev.target).parents('li[data-section]').
    attr('data-status',null);
        });
      }
      });
    </script>
```

With this code we check if the browser doesn't support touch events (and therefore doesn't support the :hover behavior we need) and then, if true, we add a data-status='selected' attribute to the element of the first-level menu that has been clicked by the user.

To achieve this result, we used a very interesting library that we'll cover in detail in the next chapter: Modernizr (http://modernizr.com/). This library contains some methods that check the presence of most of the HTML5 and CSS3 features (for example, Modernizr.touch) returning true or false.

Additionally, each feature is also expressed in the form of a class attached to the html element. For example, if there is a support for touch events, the html element receives the class touch; otherwise it receives the class no-touch.

To complete this step, all we need to do is restrict the selector that uses :hover to touch-enabled devices only and take care of the new data-status="selected" attribute. To do so, we need to change a little the nav > ul > li > .item:hover + ul selector within application_mobile.css, as follows:

```
nav > ul > li[data-status="selected"] > .item + ul,
.touch nav > ul > li > .item:hover + ul
```

Final adjustments

We can now conclude this project by adding some more enhancements with the
`:after` and `:before` pseudo-selectors. So let's add this final touch to `application_mobile.css`:

```
nav > ul > li > .item:after,
nav > ul > li > ul > li.cursor:before{
   content: '>';
   display: block;
   font-size: 1em;
   line-height: 3em;
   position: absolute;
   top: 0px;
   text-shadow: 1px 1px 0px rgba(0,0,0,0.5);
   font-weight: bold;
   color: #fff;
}

nav > ul > li > ul > li.cursor:before{
   content: '<';
   left: 15px;
}

nav > ul > li > .item:after{
   right: 15px;
}
```

Every time we use CSS-generated content, we have to remember that the content
we inject is not handled by a screen reader; so we have to take care of that either by
injecting only non-essential content, such as in this case, or by providing a fallback
mechanism.

Ok, let's reload the project in our mobile browser simulator for the last time to see the
final result:

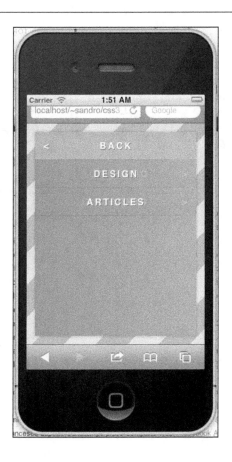

Improving speed

If we want to improve the speed of the "slide in" animation, one of the most effective change we can implement is removing transparency from the background. To do this, we have to add some more CSS to `application_mobile.css` in order to overwrite the settings inherited from the desktop version:

```
nav > ul > li > ul{
  background-color: rgb(117,189,70);
  background-image: none;
}

nav > ul > li[data-section=interests] > ul{
  background-color: rgb(186, 99, 195);
}

nav > ul > li[data-section=portfolio] > ul{
  background-color: rgb(70, 141, 189);
}
```

Implementing in older browsers

We have been careful while developing this project, so even if the animations and the gradients are not supported by older browsers, the basic structure works perfectly. The following is a screenshot taken from Internet Explorer 8:

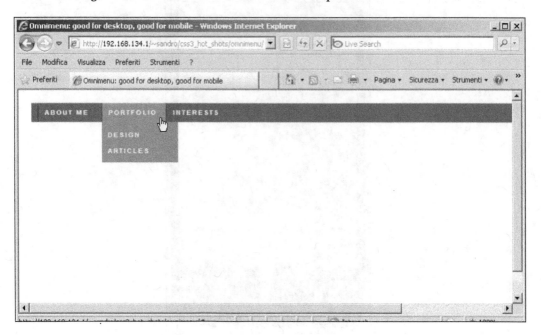

Summary

In this chapter, we experimented with the power of media queries and we started discovering animations and transitions. We also discovered the differences between `display:inline-block` and floating elements, and we started collecting a few tips on mobile performances. Of course we will have time to dig deeper into these new features in the following chapters, to discover many other interesting CSS3 properties.

However, now it's time to turn the page and start working on a new interesting project involving handling infographics!

4
Zooming User Interface

In this chapter, we'll learn how to create a simple **ZUI**. This acronym stands for a **zooming user interface**; a graphical environment where users can change the scale of the viewed area in order to see more or less detail. For this project, we'll create a ZUI to let users move and explore an **infographic**, which is a visual graphic representation of data, information, or knowledge. The project we are going to build combines many CSS3 features, such as transitions, transformations, and Flexible Box Layout. It also introduces SVG and the various methods we can use to embed them in an HTML page. Additionally, as an extra challenge, we will also enable our page to perform on older browsers and will explore clever ways to accomplish this task.

The following is a preview of the topics discussed in this chapter:

* Infographics
* Flexible Box Layout
* Polyfills
* Embedding SVG
* Modernizr
* The :target pseudo-selector
* CSS3 transforms
* Targeting SVG with CSS
* Graceful degradation

Infographics

Infographics are rapidly changing the way we consume information by creating graphical representations that aggregate data or show flows, and are able to display a great quantity of knowledge in a very intuitive and easy-to-use way. A great source of information about this topic is the blog, FlowingData (`http://flowingdata.com/`).

For this project, we will use the following stunning infographic created by Oxigenio, an Italian-based company (`http://www.officinastrategia.it`):

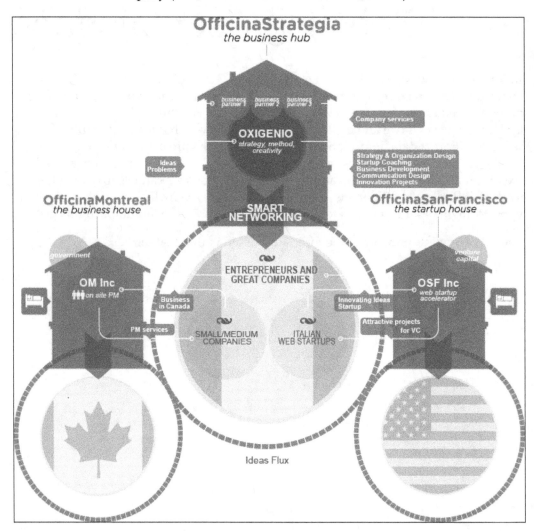

We want to reserve most of the browser's viewport area for this amazing infographic, except for a sidebar, 200 px wide, which contains some commands we'll see in a moment. First let's define some basic HTML in an `index.html` file:

```
<!doctype html>
<html>
  <head>
    <meta charset="utf-8">
    <meta http-equiv="X-UA-Compatible" content="IE=edge" />
    <title> A ZUI for an infographic</title>
    <link rel="stylesheet" type="text/css"
href="http://yui.yahooapis.com/3.5.0/build/cssreset/
cssreset-min.css" data-noprefix>
    <link rel="stylesheet" type="text/css"
href="css/application.css">

    <script src="js/modernizr.js"></script>
    <script src="js/prefixfree.js"></script>

  </head>
  <body>
    <section id="infographic">
      <header>
        <h1>a cool infographic</h1>
      </header>
      <article>

      </article>
    </section>
  </body>
</html>
```

For this project, we use the `modernizr.js` and `prefixfree.js` files. So let's create a `js` directory under the root folder of our project and download them to there from their respective websites (`http://modernizr.com/downloads/modernizr-latest.js` and `http://leaverou.github.com/prefixfree/`).

Next we have to prepare a `css` folder and create an empty `application.css` in it.

The HTML structure we defined so far is quite simple and minimalistic: a `header` element and an `article` element surrounded by a `section` element. Now we want to place the `header` element on the left side with a fixed width of 200 px, and tell the `article` element to cover the remaining portion of the screen.

We can achieve this element disposition with a variety of techniques. For the purpose of this book, we're going to use CSS3 Flexible Box Layout.

Implementing Flexible Box Layout

CSS2.1 defined four layout modes: block, inline, tabular, and positioned. CSS3 has added some new layout modes, and one of them is **Flexible Box Layout**. This new mode is activated by a new value we can give to the `display` statement, and can be configured through a whole new set of properties.

The basic idea behind this new layout mode is that within a container element (for example, our `section` element) we can specify the direction we want our inner elements to be displayed in. So if we say `horizontal` then the elements will flow from left to right, and if we say `vertical` they'll be positioned one below the other, top to bottom.

Then we can decide the size of each of the elements either by using fixed dimensions or by defining a grow factor.

 When a new space is available within the container, the elements increase their width proportionally to their grow factors.

Enough talk! Let's create a small demo to test this out:

```
<!doctype html>
<html>
  <head>
    <meta charset="utf-8">
    <meta http-equiv="X-UA-Compatible" content="IE=edge" />
    <title> A ZUI for an infographic</title>
    <link rel="stylesheet" type="text/css"
href="http://yui.yahooapis.com/3.5.0/build/cssreset/
cssreset-min.css">

    <style>
      ul{
        width: 500px;
        height: 200px;
        display: box;
        counter-reset: anchors;
        box-orient: horizontal;
        border: 1px solid black;
      }
      li{
        text-align: center;
        line-height: 200px;
        display: block;
        box-flex: 1;
```

```
          counter-increment: anchors;
        }
        li:hover{
          box-flex: 2;
        }
        li:nth-child(2n){
          background: #ddd;
        }
        li:before{
          content: counter(anchors);
        }
      </style>

      <script src="js/prefixfree.js"></script>
    </head>
    <body>
      <ul>
        <li></li>
        <li></li>
        <li></li>
        <li></li>
        <li></li>
      </ul>
    </body>
</html>
```

We can see how the li elements within the ul element start with the same width, which is exactly one-fifth of the width of the containing element. This is because they all have the same grow factor specified by the property box-flex, which makes them divide the available space equally. When we hover our mouse over one of the li elements, we change the box-flex value of the element; we hover over to 2 that makes its width twice as long as the others. The following is a screenshot with the page just loaded:

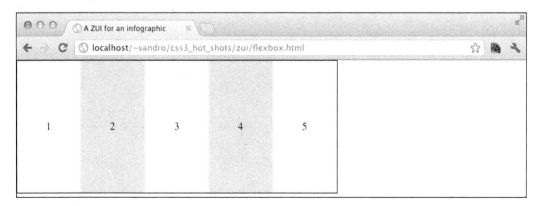

The following is a screenshot while hovering over an element:

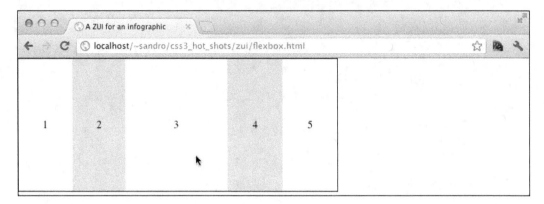

By changing the direction property (box-orient) from horizontal to vertical, we can observe the same behavior on the opposite axis. Due to the structure of this specific example, we also have to modify line-height to remove the 200px height we have set:

```
ul{
    box-orient: vertical;
}
li{
    line-height: normal;
}
```

The following is the screenshot that shows the result:

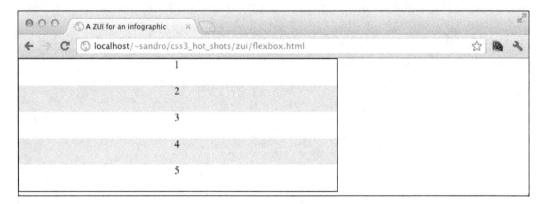

Defining the basic structure

Now that we have the basics to create the structure of our project, we need to define a horizontal direction within the `section` element, and then set the `header` element's width to a fixed value.

We have already created the `index.html` HTML in the first section of this chapter. Now let's reprint the `body` section again for clarity:

```
<body>
  <section id="infographic">
    <header>
      <h1>a cool infographic</h1>
    </header>
    <article>

    </article>
  </section>
</body>
```

We can start adding the following instructions to `application.css`:

```
html, body{
  height: 100%;
}
body{
  overflow: hidden;
font-family: sans-serif;
}
section{
  display: box;
  box-orient: horizontal;
  height: 100%;
  width: 100%;
  overflow: hidden;
}
header{
  width: 200px;
  background: rgb(181, 65, 71);
}
article{
  background-color: rgb(204, 204, 204);
  background-image:
    repeating-linear-gradient(bottom left, rgb(204, 204, 204) 0px,
    rgb(204, 204, 204) 20px,
    rgb(210, 210, 210) 20px, rgb(210, 210, 210) 40px);
  box-flex: 1;
  overflow: hidden;
  position: relative;
}
```

We've added a little more instructions than in the previous example because we also want the `section` element to cover the whole browser's viewport. Additionally, we should prevent the display of a vertical scroll bar because the only navigation mechanisms must be the ones offered by the ZUI. So we've added an `overflow: hidden` property to both `section` and `article`.

If we now load the project in a browser that supports CSS3, we can appreciate the result:

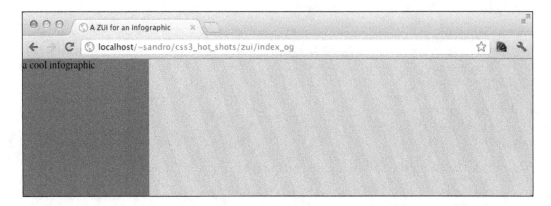

The Flexible Box Layout Module specification is evolving rapidly, and currently none of the web browsers support all of the specs. Our implementation corresponds to the following document published on July 23, 2009:

```
http://www.w3.org/TR/2009/
WD-css3-flexbox-20090723/
```

Adding Polyfills

For the first time since the beginning of this book, we are using CSS3 to define the structure of our page. This means we cannot simply rely on graceful degradation to support older browsers because it would compromise the whole structure of the project. Instead, we're going to look for some JavaScript libraries that are able to emulate the behavior we have implemented. This, of course, can lead to some problems if the user's browser is missing both JavaScript support and Flexible Box Layout, but at least we can hope that the number of such users is pretty low.

There are different types of such JavaScript libraries, categorized by how much extra work is required to obtain the same result as the native implementation:

- **Generic libraries**: Generic libraries don't allow the developer to obtain exactly the same result, but give him/her some tools to code an alternative implementation of the solution.

- **Shims**: Shims allow the developer to mimic the native implementation perfectly, but achieving it requires an extra cost in terms of work.

- **Polyfills**: Polyfills are the best ones. These libraries read our code, detect the unsupported features, and implement the required JavaScript workaround without the need to add extra code.

We need to find a polyfill that emulates Flexible Box Layout Module. We can start our search from the following page, created and kept by the authors of Modernizr that lists all the polyfills they have tested and found to work:

`https://github.com/Modernizr/Modernizr/wiki/HTML5-Cross-Browser-Polyfills`

After scrolling down the page, we find Flexie, which claims to add support to Flexible Box Layout for older browsers (up to IE6). All we have to do is download the library, `flexie.js`, to our `js` folder (it is also available from GitHub at `https://github.com/doctyper/flexie`, within the `src` folder).

Let's modify our `index.html` file by adding the following lines just before the `</body>` tag:

```
<!-- Adding older browser's support -->
<script
src="http://ajax.googleapis.com/ajax/libs/jquery/1.7.2/
jquery.min.js"></script>
<script src="js/flexie.js"></script>
```

Now we can test if everything went well by loading our project in a browser that doesn't support CSS3 Flexible Box Layout. The following is a screenshot taken from IE8:

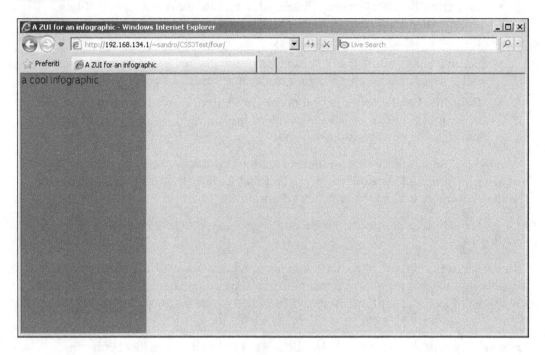

As we see from the output, there's no striped background but the overall structure is well preserved.

Adding a polyfill to a project inevitably increases its level of complexity. Polyfills are almost always able to emulate the CSS3 feature they are built for, but in a way that obviously differs from the native implementation. It might be that a polyfill needs to inject extra elements to our page, or to add CSS properties. So it's a good rule of thumb to add these libraries earlier, during the development of our pages and to test them often in order to catch conflicts between the developing pages and libraries.

Embedding SVG

We'd like to use **Scalable Vector Graphics (SVG)** instead of a raster image where supported. We're building a ZUI so our infographic needs to be zoomed, and using a vector graphic allows us to preserve the quality of the object. Vector images, in fact, are size independent and thus don't get pixelated when scaled.

 More information about vector images and SVG can be found on Wikipedia at `http://en.wikipedia.org/wiki/Vector_graphics`.

There are three ways to embed an SVG:

- As an `<object>` element. This is the most supported way of adding SVG. However, it is limited in a sense that the SVG is treated like an external element and therefore cannot be manipulated through JavaScript (except for some obvious properties, such as `width` and `height`).

- As a value for CSS where an image is required.

- Directly into our HTML code. This approach offers the most interaction available between the SVG and the page. As we'll see later in this chapter, we can interact with the vector graphic directly from CSS, or even from JavaScript.

Let's go for the third way because we want our CSS to be able to affect part of the SVG graphic. First of all, let's create a `div` element that is going to act as a container for our SVG element within the `<article>` we created earlier in this chapter:

```
<article>
<div class="panel">

  <!-- place here the svg content -->

</div>
</article>
```

Next, we can use jQuery to load the SVG file from the `img` folder directly into the container we just created by adding a few lines to our `index.html` file, after the `script` tags we wrote earlier:

```
<script>
  $(document).ready(function(){
    $('div.panel').load('img/infographic.svg' );
  });
</script>
</body>
```

In these lines, we first ask jQuery to wait until the DOM is ready, and then to load the content of our SVG file inside the `div` element with the `.panel` class.

Now we can add a bit of CSS to center the `div` element both vertically and horizontally in the containing `article`.

This can be weird because only Webkit browsers and IE9+ seem to accept a container with size `100%`, so we have to discriminate between these browsers and the others. So let's add the following instructions to `application.css`:

```
div.panel{
  width: 572px;
  height: 547px;
}

.-webkit- div.panel,
.-ms- div.panel {
  width: 100%;
  height: 100%;
}

img.panel{
  display: block;
  position: absolute;
  top: 50%; left: 50%;
  margin-top: -282px;
  margin-left: -273px;
}

html:not(.-webkit-):not(.-ms-) div.panel{
  display: block;
  position: absolute;
  top: 50%; left: 50%;
  margin-top: -282px;
  margin-left: -273px;
}
```

We have now covered all the possible cases:

- We used Prefix Free's ability to add an extra class to the `<html>` element to detect Webkit and Microsoft browsers, and set the container size to `100%` for these browsers in order to obtain an SVG as big as the container permits

- If the browser is not one of those discussed in the previous item, we align the SVG centrally and set a fixed size

- If there is an image instead of the SVG (we'll see in a moment how we can handle this), we do basically the same thing as in the previous item.

If we now reload the project in our browser, we can see the display of the SVG:

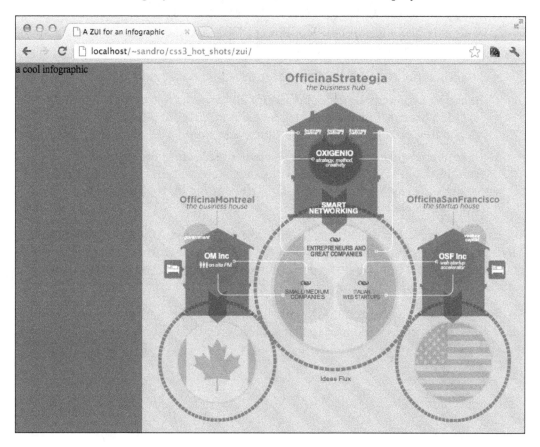

Due to the fact that we're using AJAX, we need a proper web server to try this project. Just double-clicking on the `index.html` file won't generate the expected results. Refer to the *Preface* section of the book to get more information on how to install a web server.

Of course there are browsers that don't support SVG. IE8 is among them, so we need to find a solution in order to keep our project enjoyable on these browsers too.

Taking advantage of Modernizr

We have already had a glimpse of Modernizr in the last chapter, it's a library that does plenty of things, some of which are listed as follows:

- It adds support for new HTML5 tags in older browsers.
- It exposes some methods in JavaScript allowing us to test for a certain CSS3/HTML5 feature. For example, `Modernizr.multiplebg` returns `true` or `false` depending on the support of multiple backgrounds.
- It adds some classes to the `<html>` element reflecting the support of certain CSS3/HTML5 features. For example, `<html class="multiplebg">` or `<html class="no-multiplebg">` depending on the support of multiple backgrounds.

We have already added this library to our project. However, if not properly tuned, Modernizr performs all the tests to detect the supported features even if we're not going to use them. To enhance the performance of the library, we can select which tests we want it to perform.

To do that, we have to click on the download page of Modernizr (`http://modernizr.com/download/`) and check only the features we're going to use this library for.

For this project, we need to test for inline SVG support. The following is a screenshot with the checkboxes on the right-hand side checked:

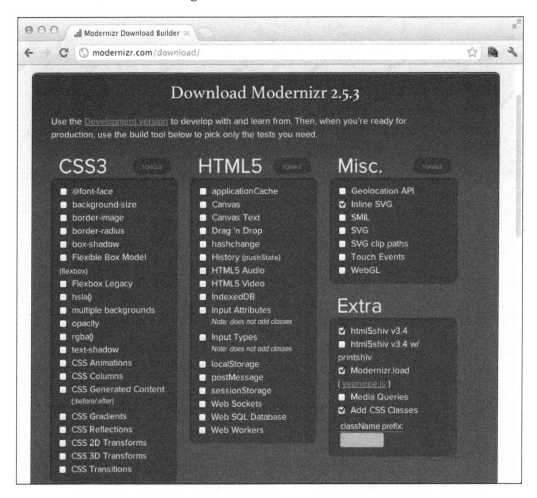

Next we click on the **Generate!** button, and then on the **Download** button to download and overwrite the `modernizr.js` file we have in our project.

We may now check the generated HTML code for our project and see how the `html` elements get enriched by an `inlinesvg` class if the browser supports inline SVG, or a `no-inlinesvg` class otherwise.

 You can check the generated HTML code using the browser's development console. If using Google Chrome, for example, press *Ctrl + Shift + I* (on Windows and Linux), or press *Command + Option + I* (on Mac).

We're now going to implement an alternative to the SVG graphic using a plain image; and then, by taking advantage of the class provided to us by Modernizr, switch between one or the other depending upon the browser's support. So let's first add a small HTML snippet to `index.html` just before the `</article>` tag:

```
<img class="panel" src="img/infographic.png">
```

Then we need to modify our `application.css`:

```
.no-inlinesvg div.panel{
  display: none;
}

.inlinesvg img.panel{
  display: none;
}
```

If we now reload the project in IE8, we can see how everything is handled correctly:

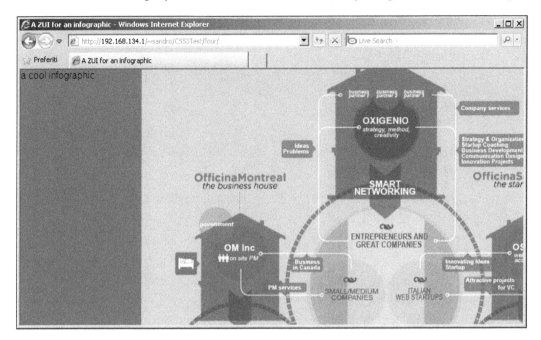

The :target pseudo-selector

Now we can start adding some interaction to our project. What we want is to expose some controls in the `<header>` sidebar that, when clicked, zoom to a defined area of the infographic.

To achieve this, we are going to take advantage of a new CSS3 pseudo-selector: `:target`. It gets activated when an anchor becomes the target of the current URL. Let's create a small example to try this out:

```
<!doctype html>
<html>
  <head>
    <meta charset="utf8">
    <title> :target test</title>
    <link rel="stylesheet" type="text/css"
href="http://yui.yahooapis.com/3.5.0/build/cssreset/
cssreset-min.css">
```

```
<style>
a[id]{
  display: block;
  width: 100px;
  height: 100px;
  text-align: center;
  line-height: 100px;
  margin: 10px;
  background: gray;
}
a:target{
  background: yellow;
}
</style>

<script src="js/prefixfree.js"></script>
</head>
<body>
  <a href="#one"> light 1 </a>
  <a href="#two"> light 2 </a>
  <a id="one" name="one"> one </a>
  <a id="two" name="two"> two </a>
</body>
</html>
```

In the previous example, we basically say that when an a element becomes the target of the current URL, its background color must turn yellow. The following screenshot shows the result (notice the URL):

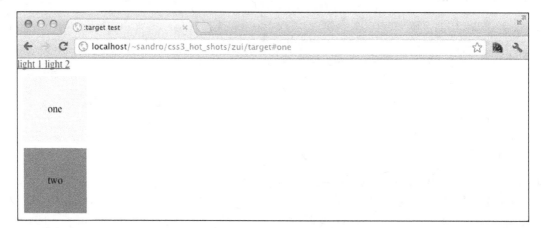

Now we need a set of a elements containing the command we want the user to be able to execute. So let's add a `nav` element within the `header` element in our `index.html` file:

```
<nav>
  <ul>
    <li><a href="#italy">Italy</a></li>
    <li><a href="#montreal">Montreal</a></li>
    <li><a href="#sanfrancisco">San Francisco</a></li>
    <li><a href="#">Whole view</a></li>
  </ul>
</nav>
```

Next, we can style these commands with a few CSS instructions in our `application.css` file:

```
nav, ul, li{
  width: 100%;
}

h1{
  font-size: 16px;
  text-transform: uppercase;
  letter-spacing: -1px;
  font-weight: bold;
  line-height: 30px;
  text-align: center;
  padding: 10px 0 10px 0;
  color: rgb(255,255,255);
  background: rgb(85, 85, 85);
  margin-bottom: 10px;
}

li, li a{
  display: block;
  height: 30px;
  line-height: 30px;
}

li a{
  color: rgb(255,255,255);
  text-decoration: none;
  font-weight: bold;
  padding-left: 20px;
}

li a:hover{
  text-decoration: underline;
}
```

If we reload the project, we can see the result:

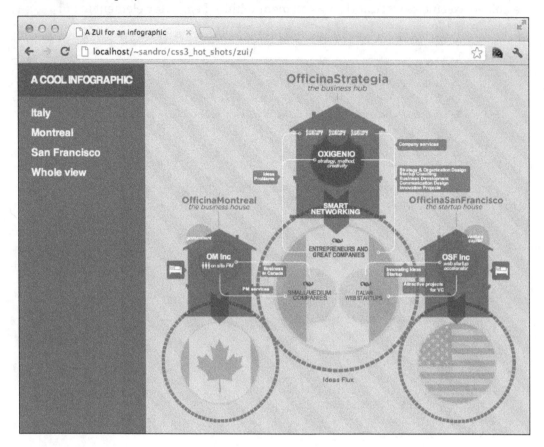

Adding some anchors

Now we need to place the a elements that are targets of the commands we just implemented. And here comes a small trick: if we put these elements on the top of our page and then we hide them, we can use proximity selectors (+ and ~) to match the elements that follow them and be able to virtually reach every other element in the page.

So, let's start by adding an a element for each command we have specified, just below the body element of our index.html file:

```
<a id="italy" name="italy"></a>
<a id="montreal" name="montreal"></a>
<a id="sanfrancisco" name="sanfrancisco"></a>
```

Good! Now if we want to change the `header` background color when the **Italy** command has been clicked, we can add a simple line to our CSS:

```
a[id="italy"]:target ~ section header{
  background: green;
}
```

Of course we don't want to do that, but by using the same principle we can trigger some changes to the infographic. First we have to learn about transformations.

CSS3 transforms

We are going to explore a whole new set of properties with the goal of being able to arbitrarily scale an element using CSS. This is the last core technique we need to learn to complete the ZUI, and the properties involved are called **CSS3 transforms**.

With CSS3 transforms we can apply some modifiers to the elements on a page, namely:

- `translateX(x)`, `translateY(y)`, and `translate(x,y)`: These modifiers move the element along one or both axes by a distance specified by the x and y variables (in px)

- `rotate(deg)`: It rotates the element by the value specified by the deg variable, which must be expressed in grades (from 0 to 360 degrees)

- `scaleX(s)`, `scaleY(s)`, and `scale(s, [s])`: It scales the element of the value specified by a scale factor s where a scale of 1 corresponds to keeping the element at the same size

- `skewX(k)` and `skewY(k)`: It applies a skew transformation by the given k angle expressed in grades (from 0 to 360 degrees)

There's also a `matrix` modifier that accepts six parameters and lets us define a transformation matrix. More information about the `matrix` modifier can be found at `http://www.w3.org/TR/SVG/coords.html#TransformMatrixDefined`.

Let's experiment with these modifiers in a small demo:

```
<!doctype html>
<html>
  <head>
    <meta charset="utf-8">
    <meta http-equiv="X-UA-Compatible" content="IE=edge" />
    <title>transform test</title>
    <link rel="stylesheet" type="text/css"
```

```
href="http://yui.yahooapis.com/3.5.0/build/cssreset/
cssreset-min.css">

    <style>
    div{
       width: 100px;
       height: 100px;
       background: green;
       margin: 30px auto;
    }
    div:first-child{
       transform: translateX(100px);
    }
    div:nth-child(2){
       transform: rotate(45deg);
    }
    div:nth-child(3){
       transform: scale(2);
       background: red;
    }
    div:nth-child(4){
       transform: skewX(45deg);
    }
    div:last-child{
       transform: skewY(45deg) scale(1.2) rotate(45deg);
    }
    </style>

    <script src="js/prefixfree.js"></script>
  </head>
  <body>
    <div>translate</div>
    <div>rotate</div>
    <div>scale</div>
    <div>skew</div>
    <div>mixed</div>
  </body>
</html>
```

As you can see, transformations can be combined in order to obtain some interesting results. The following is a screenshot of this demo running in a CSS3-compliant browser:

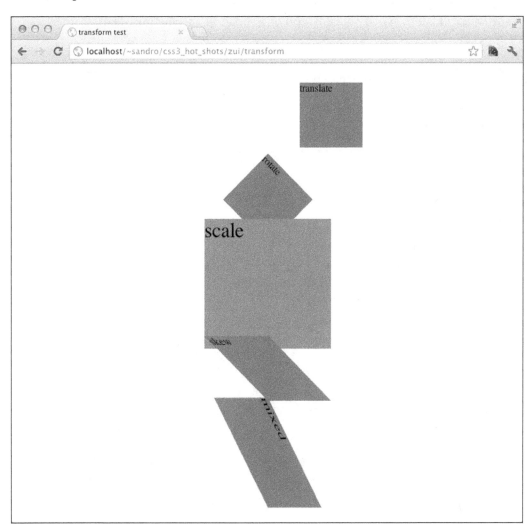

 Another good feature to note is the fact that the element position is calculated *before* the transformation is applied. A proof of this is the fact that the scaled div element doesn't move the others down, but simply overlaps them.

Applying transformations

Now we only need to put together what we have just learned, and transform the infographic in response to a click of one of the commands. To have a smooth transformation, let's specify a transition of 1 second to all the transform properties in `application.css`:

```css
.panel{
    transition: transform 1s;
}

/*
Now we can add these few instructions to trigger the transform when
corresponding anchor became target of the current URL:
*/

a[id='italy']:target ~ section div.panel {
   transform: scale(2) translateY(15%);
   -ms-transform: scale(2) translateY(15%);
}

a[id='montreal']:target ~ section div.panel{
   transform: scale(1.8) translate(24%, -21%);
   -ms-transform: scale(1.8) translate(24%, -21%);
}

a[id='sanfrancisco']:target ~ section div.panel{
   transform: scale(1.8) translate(-24%, -21%);
   -ms-transform: scale(1.8) translate(-24%, -21%);
}
```

Good! Let's reload the project in a browser:

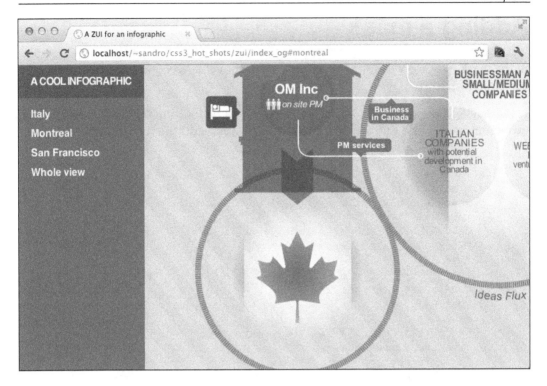

Flashing issues

All of the latest Chrome versions (up to version 18 at the time of writing) switch between CPU and GPU-accelerated graphics when some CSS properties are applied (transitions are among them). This could generate a flash on the screen if the computer is not fast enough to handle it. One solution is to force Chrome to apply a GPU-accelerated property when the page loads. In this solution, the 3D transform properties we'll see in the next few chapters come in handy, so we can add a null `translateZ` property to the `body` element as follows:

```
body{
   -webkit-transform: translateZ(0);
}
```

However, we have to remember that this solution lowers the quality of the SVG because Chrome doesn't seem to refine graphics after a `transform` property while accelerated. Additionally, 3D transform properties such as the one we just used should be treated with caution on mobile environments as they are memory intensive.

Adding a mask

We might want to add a small description mask for each of the zoom areas available. In the mask, we also want the user to be able to move between the zoomed areas using small arrows.

First of all let's define the HTML needed: there will be four masks, one for each of the three commands, and one for the central area. We can add the required markup just after the `</section>` tag:

```
<div id="mask">
  <div data-detail="italy">
    <span>Help text. Click the arrows to explore more.</span>
    <menu>
      <a role="button" aria-label="move down"
href="#italy2">&#x25BC;</a>
    </menu>
  </div>
  <div data-detail="italy2">
    <span>Help text. Click the arrows to explore more.</span>
    <menu>
      <a role="button" aria-label="move left"
href="#montreal">&#x25C4;</a>
      <a role="button" aria-label="move up"
href="#italy">&#x25B2;</a><a role="button" aria-label="move right"
href="#sanfrancisco">&#x25BA;</a>
    </menu>
  </div>
  <div data-detail="montreal">
    <span>Help text. Click the arrows to explore more.</span>
    <menu>
      <a role="button" aria-label="move right"
href="#italy2">&#x25BA;</a>
    </menu>
  </div>
  <div data-detail="sanfrancisco">
    <span>Help text. Click the arrows to explore more.</span>
    <menu>
      <a role="button" aria-label="move left"
href="#italy2">&#x25C4;</a>
    </menu>
  </div>
</div>
```

Now we have to place the `#mask` element just below the bottom line of the viewport, and activate it when one of the commands is triggered. So let's write the following instructions in `application.css`:

```css
#mask{
  position: absolute;
  padding-top: 5px;
  font-size: 18px;
  font-weight: bold;
  height: 50px;
  color: rgb(255,255,255);
  background-color: rgb(0,0,0);
  background-color: rgba(0,0,0,0.8);
  text-align: center;
  bottom: -55px;
  left: 201px;
  right: 0;
}

#mask menu{
  position: absolute;
  padding: 0; margin: 0;
  bottom: 4px;
  left: 0;
  right: 0;
  text-align: center;
}

#mask div{
  display: none;
}

#mask a{
  text-decoration: none;
  color: rgb(255,255,255);
  padding: 0 10px;
}

a[id='montreal']:target ~ #mask div[data-detail="montreal"],
a[id='italy2']:target ~ #mask div[data-detail="italy2"],
a[id='italy']:target ~ #mask div[data-detail="italy"],
a[id='sanfrancisco']:target ~ #mask
div[data-detail="sanfrancisco"]{
  display: block;
}

a[id='italy']:target ~ #mask,
a[id='italy2']:target ~ #mask,
a[id='montreal']:target ~ #mask,
a[id='sanfrancisco']:target ~ #mask{
  transition: bottom 1s;
  bottom: 0;
}
```

In the highlighted chunk of code, we instructed the browser to:

- Hide the `#mask` element below the browser bottom line
- Hide all the `div` elements within the `#mask` element
- Show only the `div` element within the `#mask` element corresponding to the targeted `a` element
- Reveal the `#mask` element when one of the `a` elements is `:target`

Now we need to take care of the `italy2` anchor. So let's add another `a` element just before `<section>` in `index.html`:

```
<a id="italy2" name="italy2"></a>
```

And the corresponding CSS in `application.css`:

```
a[id='italy2']:target ~ section div.panel{
    transform: scale(2) translateY(-15%);
    -ms-transform: scale(2) translateY(-15%);
}
```

Well done! Now let's reload the project in the browser:

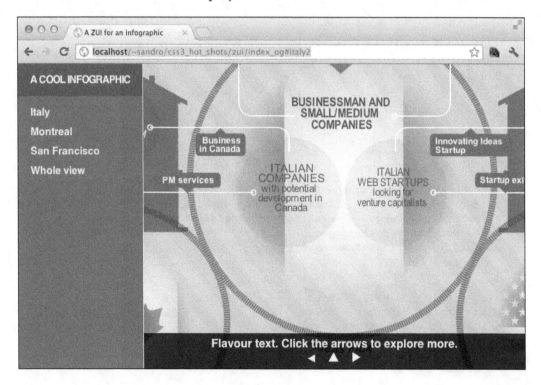

Targeting SVG with CSS

Ok, time for some final touches. What we want now is to provide a mechanism to toggle the visibility of the labels of the infographic. Due to the fact that our SVG is inline, we can turn them off by simply adding opacity: 0 to their id selector, in the same way as we would have done with plain HTML elements. So let's add the following lines to application.css:

```
#Layer_2{ /* this id is present within the SVG */
  opacity: 0;
  transition: opacity 1s;
}
```

The next step is to find a way to let the user toggle the opacity value. We can achieve this result using a checkbox and taking advantage of the :checked pseudo-selector more or less as we did with the :target one.

So, first of all let's add a checkbox just before the <section> tag in our index.html file:

```
<input type="checkbox" id="show_labels" name="show_labels">
```

And then, let's add the corresponding label just before the </ul> tag in the nav command:

```
<li><label for="show_labels"></label></li>
```

Now add the following lines to application.css:

```
#show_labels{
  display: none;
}

nav label:before{
  content: 'Click to show labels';
}

#show_labels:checked ~ section label:before{
  content: 'Click to hide labels';
}

#show_labels:checked ~ section #Layer_2{
  opacity: 1;
}

label{
  text-align: left;
  font-family: sans-serif;
  padding-left: 20px;
```

```css
    font-size: 13px;
    cursor: pointer;
}

nav label{
    display: block;
    height: 30px;
    line-height: 30px;
}

li:not(:nth-last-child(2)) a:after{
    content: " \00BB";
}

li:nth-last-child(2) a:before{
    content: "\00AB";
}
```

The following is a final screenshot of our project:

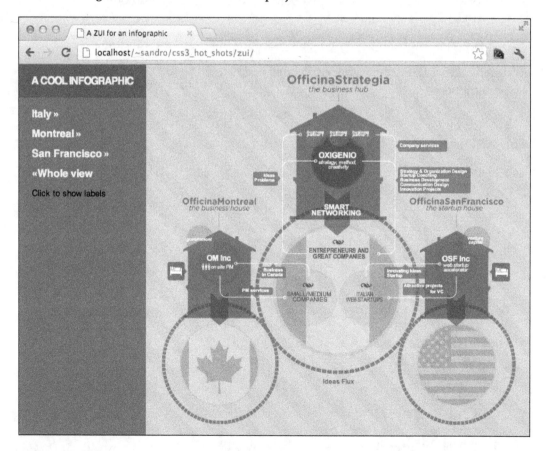

Graceful degradation

Because we added CSS transformations, things started to go wrong on older browsers. In fact, both transformations and the :target pseudo-selector are not supported on older browsers, so we have to find a valid alternative. One solution can be to listen to URL hash changes via JavaScript and use a hashchange event to add a class reflecting the current hash to both section and #mask elements. This class can then be used to trigger some CSS properties.

To be able to listen to the hashchange event on older browsers, we need a small JavaScript library. We can download it from http://benalman.com/code/projects/jquery-hashchange/docs/files/jquery-ba-hashchange-js.html, rename it to jquery.hashchange.js, and place it in our js folder. Next we have to replace our copy of Modernizr (js/modernizr.js) with a new one that also includes the test for **multiple backgrounds**. To achieve this, we can use the same procedure as discussed earlier.

Now we need to insert this library and then add some small JavaScript code just before the </body> tag:

```
<script src="js/jquery.hashchange.js"></script>
<script>
  $(document).ready(function(){
/* we check for multiblegbs support because browsers who do support
multiple backgrounds surely support also the features we need */
    if(!Modernizr.multiplebgs){
      if(window.location.hash.substring(1) != "")
        window.location.href =
window.location.href.replace(window.location.hash,'');
      jQuery(window).hashchange(function(e){
        $('section, #mask').
removeClass().addClass(window.location.hash.substring(1));
      });
    }
  });
</script>
```

Good! Now we can emulate the `transform` property by varying the width, height, and position of the `img.panel` element. Additionally, we can also use the class we added dynamically with JavaScript to show and hide the `#mask` element.

```css
.no-inlinesvg #mask{
  left: 0px;
}

.no-inlinesvg label{
  display: none;
}

#mask.montreal, #mask.sanfrancisco, #mask.italy, #mask.italy2{
  bottom: 0px;
}

#mask.montreal div[data-detail="montreal"],
#mask.italy2 div[data-detail="italy2"],
#mask.italy div[data-detail="italy"],
#mask.sanfrancisco div[data-detail="sanfrancisco"]{
  display: block;
}

section.italy img.panel{
  top: 60%; left: 25%;
  width: 1000px;
  height: 1000px;
}

section.italy2 img.panel{
  top: 0%; left: 25%;
  width: 1000px;
  height: 1000px;
}

section.montreal img.panel{
  top: -10%; left: 50%;
  width: 1000px;
  height: 1000px;
}
```

```
section.sanfrancisco img.panel{
  top: -10%; left: 0%;
  width: 1000px;
  height: 1000px;
}
```

The following screenshot shows the final result:

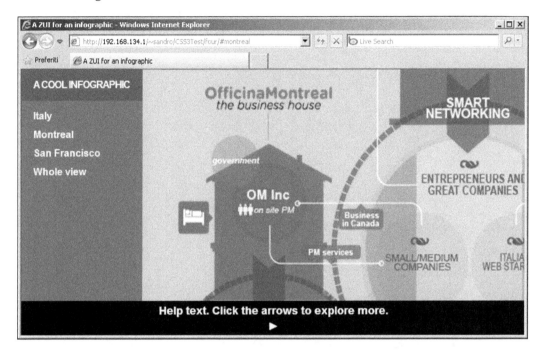

Summary

In this chapter, we learned how to deal with CSS3 properties that structurally affect our page. We also discovered transformations, and some cool ways to interact with SVG. In the next chapter, we'll discuss how to enhance an image gallery.

5
An Image Gallery

Image galleries are nowadays a common component of a website. In this chapter, we'll discover how we can implement a range of transition effects and several navigation modes using *only* CSS properties. We'll start by implementing a basic transition effect using a series of images, then we'll develop a pure CSS structure to let the user select his preferred navigation mode and transition effect and, finally, we'll add more complex transition effects. The following is a list of the topics we'll cover in this chapter:

- A basic gallery HTML structure
- Implementing opacity transition
- Implementing slide transition
- 3D transformations
- Adding the slideshow mode
- Creating previous and next arrow
- CSS preprocessors

Preparing the structure

As in the previous chapters, we will first define a basic HTML structure on which we will build our project. So let's create a new folder for this project with a file named index.html containing the following code:

```
<!doctype html>
<html>
  <head>
    <meta charset="utf-8">
    <meta http-equiv="X-UA-Compatible" content="IE=edge" />
    <title>A 3D Gallery</title>
```

```html
    <link rel="stylesheet" type="text/css" href="http://yui.yahooapis.
com/3.7.3/build/cssreset/
cssreset-min.css">
    <link rel="stylesheet" type="text/css"
href="css/application.css">
    <script src="js/prefixfree.js"></script>
  </head>
  <body>
    <div>
      choose effect:
      <input type="radio" name="mode" id="opacity" checked >
      <label for="opacity">opacity</label>
      <input type="radio" name="mode" id="slidein">
      <label for="slidein">slidein</label>
      <input type="radio" name="mode" id="cube" >
      <label for="cube">cube</label>
      <br>
      choose mode:
      <input type="radio" name="controls" id="animate">
      <label for="animate">animate</label>
      <input type="radio" name="controls" id="bullets" checked>
      <label for="bullets">bullets</label>
      <input type="radio" name="controls" id="arrows">
      <label for="arrows">arrows</label>

      <a id="picture1" name="picture1"></a>
      <a id="picture2" name="picture2"></a>
      <a id="picture3" name="picture3"></a>
      <a id="picture4" name="picture4"></a>
      <a id="picture5" name="picture5"></a>
      <section>
        <ul>
          <li>
            <figure id="shot1"></figure>
          </li>
          <li>
            <figure id="shot2"></figure>
          </li>
          <li>
            <figure id="shot3"></figure>
          </li>
          <li>
            <figure id="shot4"></figure>
          </li>
          <li>
            <figure id="shot5"></figure>
          </li>
```

```
      </ul>
      <span>
        <a href="#picture1" ></a>
        <a href="#picture2" ></a>
        <a href="#picture3" ></a>
        <a href="#picture4" ></a>
        <a href="#picture5" ></a>
      </span>
    </section>
  </div>
 </body>
</html>
```

As in the previous chapters, we are using the Yahoo! Reset CSS stylesheet as well as Lea Verou's Prefix Free library. You can copy `prefixfree.js` from the previous chapter's example, or download it from `http://leaverou.github.com/prefixfree/`.

The structure we defined contains a few radio buttons divided into two groups: `mode` and `controls`. In this project, we'll learn how to change the behavior of our gallery to reflect the choices made by our users. The default settings, the ones we're going to implement first, concern an opacity transition and a bullet-based navigation system.

Next there are anchors in a quantity equal to the number of images we want to display. Then, within a `section` element, we have a `figure` element for each image, and an `a` element pointing to the anchors previously defined.

What we're going to implement consists of activating a particular image when the corresponding `a` element is pressed. To do so, we'll use the already introduced `:target` pseudo-selector in conjunction with some other little useful tricks, but first we have to spend a little time defining the base CSS structure.

Applying the basic CSS

First of all, we have to center our project in the middle of the browser's viewport and then style the radio buttons a bit. To do this we write a few lines of CSS in `application.css`, as follows:

```
/* == [BEGIN] General == */

body,html{
  height: 100%;
  background-image: radial-gradient(center center, white, gray);
}
```

```
body > div{
  position: absolute;
  width: 500px;
  height: 400px;
  top: 50%; left: 50%;
  margin-left: -250px;
  margin-top: -200px;
  text-align: center;
  font-family: sans-serif;
  font-size: 13px;
  color: #444;
  line-height: 1.5;
}

section{
  margin-top: 20px;
  width: 500px;
  height: 390px;
  position: relative;
}

section > ul{
  width: 500px;
  height: 390px;
  position: relative;
}

input{
  width: 20px;
}

/* == [END] General == */
```

Good! Now let's assign the corresponding image to each figure element:

```
/* == [BEGIN] Pics == */

section figure {
  position: absolute;
  top: 0px; left: 0px;
  width: 500px; height: 370px;
  padding: 0px; margin: 0px;
  background-position: center center;
}

#shot1{
  background-image: url('../img/picture1.jpg');
}
```

```
#shot2{
  background-image: url('../img/picture2.jpg');
}

#shot3{
  background-image: url('../img/picture3.jpg');
}

#shot4{
  background-image: url('../img/picture4.jpg');
}

#shot5{
  background-image: url('../img/picture5.jpg');
}

/* == [END] Pics == */
```

 Please note that in a real-world example, we would probably have inserted these images dynamically via a `style` attribute.

Now we can test the success of this setup phase using a CSS3-compliant browser. At this point we haven't added any behavior to the radio buttons, so we expect only to see the image within `#shot5` without any kind of interaction or animation.

Styling the bullets

Let's start applying some style to the a elements. We created the bullets first because they are the default representation. Our bullets will be visible as a set of hollow, clickable circles below the image as are often found in online slideshows. We can use some rounded borders for the circles and apply a background rule when the element has been clicked upon. To intercept this state, we'll use the :target pseudo-selector on the corresponding a element that we have inserted at the top of our page.

```
/* == [BEGIN] Span == */

section > span > a{
    display: inline-block;
    text-decoration: none;
    color: black;
    font-size: 1px;
    padding: 3px;
    border: 1px solid black;
    border-radius: 4px;
    font-weight: bold;
}

section > span{
    position: absolute;
    bottom: 0px;
    left: 0px;
    right: 0px;
    text-align: center;
}

a[name=picture1]:target ~ section a[href="#picture1"],
a[name=picture2]:target ~ section a[href="#picture2"],
a[name=picture3]:target ~ section a[href="#picture3"],
a[name=picture4]:target ~ section a[href="#picture4"],
a[name=picture5]:target ~ section a[href="#picture5"]{
    background: #111;
}

/* == [END] Span == */
```

We decided to set the bullets to display:inline-block in order to benefit from the space that this property injects between the elements when some space is left between their tags, as we saw in *Chapter 3, Omni Menu.*

Next we used the `:target` pseudo-selector in conjunction with the proximity one, `~`, to define a rule that matches the bullet that points to the current anchor.

Now everything is ready and we can start working on our first transition effect: opacity.

Implementing opacity transition

The opacity effect is the simplest, all we have to do is to hide all the elements through the property `opacity:0`, except the one that corresponds to the clicked bullet. To obtain a nice fading effect, we can then specify a transition period between the two states using the `transition` property.

A trick we have to implement here is to attach this behavior only when the **opacity** radio button is selected in our settings panel. To accomplish this, we can place another selector, `#opacity:checked`, before the rule:

```
/* == [BEGIN] Opacity == */

#opacity:checked ~ section figure{
  opacity: 0;
  transition: opacity 0.4s;
}

#opacity:checked ~ a:not(:target) + a:not(:target) + a:not(:target) +
a:not(:target) + a:not(:target) ~ section #shot1,
#opacity:checked ~ a[name=picture1]:target ~ section #shot1,
#opacity:checked ~ a[name=picture2]:target ~ section #shot2,
#opacity:checked ~ a[name=picture3]:target ~ section #shot3,
#opacity:checked ~ a[name=picture4]:target ~ section #shot4,
#opacity:checked ~ a[name=picture5]:target ~ section #shot5{
  opacity: 1;
}

/* == [END] Opacity == */
```

We basically used the same trick as earlier, plus we added a rule to set `opacity:1` to the first image if no bullets are selected. To accomplish this, we used the + selector to specifically match five sequential a elements that aren't `:target`.

Well done! If we run the project in a browser, we can test the effect and notice how this works *only* if the corresponding radio button is selected.

 A final note before moving ahead, the selectors we created for this project are quite complex and, if used extensively in big applications, may introduce performance issues.

Time to implement a new effect: slide!

Implementing slide transition

A slide effect is basically a transition where one element moves outside the user's view, sliding in one direction while another moves in. To implement this effect, we have to work on two different animations: slide in and slide out. The basic idea to make this effect work is similar to the previous one, although slightly more complicated. To achieve the slide-in effect, we have to move all the pictures outside the section viewport, say `left:-500px` and then, when the corresponding bullet is clicked, take the selected picture and move it to the opposite side (`left:500px`) using an animation that then moves it to the correct position (`left:0`).

To achieve the slide-out effect, we can then use another animation that starts from
`left:0px` to `left:-500px`. The following is the complete CSS snippet:

```css
/* == [BEGIN] Slide In == */

#slidein:checked ~ section > ul{
  overflow:hidden;
}

#slidein:checked ~ section figure{
  left: -500px;
  animation-name: slideout;
  animation-duration: 1.5s;
}

#slidein:checked ~ a:not(:target) + a:not(:target) + a:not(:target) +
a:not(:target) + a:not(:target) ~ section #shot1,
#slidein:checked ~ a[name=picture1]:target ~ section #shot1,
#slidein:checked ~ a[name=picture2]:target ~ section #shot2,
#slidein:checked ~ a[name=picture3]:target ~ section #shot3,
#slidein:checked ~ a[name=picture4]:target ~ section #shot4,
#slidein:checked ~ a[name=picture5]:target ~ section #shot5{
  animation-name: slidein;
  animation-duration: 1.5s;
  left: 0px;
}

@keyframes slidein{
  0% { left: 500px; }
  100% { left: 0px; }
}

@keyframes slideout{
  0% { left: 0px; }
  100% { left: -500px; }
}

/* == [END] Slide In == */
```

We used `overflow:hidden` to hide the images outside the section viewport. The
`slideout` animation is added to all the elements except the selected one, so when
an element exits from the selected state, the animation gets activated and moves the
element to `left:-500px` smoothly.

The following is a screenshot taken from a CSS3-compliant browser (for example, Chrome, Firefox, IE10, and so on):

Now we're ready to code the third transition effect: cube! But first, in order to better understand the next step, let's spend some time introducing the basics of 3D transformations.

3D transformations

3D transformations introduce a big leap-forward in designing websites. We can now experiment with moving and animating elements such as `div`, `img`, or even `video` in a 3D space that benefits from GPU acceleration (for most browsers). The first thing we have to deal with once we decide to introduce 3D effects is the **perspective**.

The value we set for the `perspective` property specifies to the browser how to render elements with a position on the z axis equal to 0 (or not set). For example, `perspective:300px` means that an element with z = 0 (or not set) is drawn as if it is 300 px away from the viewport. This, of course, affects the way the elements are rendered when rotated.

Next comes a useful property whose purpose is to tell the browser to apply 3D transformations. This property is called `transform-style` and its value can either be `flat` or `preserve-3d`. When the value is `flat`, the elements with transformations that affect rotation on the x or y axis do not have perspective, but when the value is `preserve-3d` they actually behave like real 3D surfaces. This property also applies to all the element's children.

Finally come the transformations. Here the property to use is the same as for the 2D ones, `transform`, but there are some new keywords that can be chosen as a value.

The transformation origin is set by default to the center of the element with z = 0, but can be adjusted using the `transform-origin` property.

With these notions in mind, we can start defining the cube effect that basically operates like the slide one but, of course, taking advantage of the 3D transform mechanism.

```
/* == [BEGIN] Cube == */

#cube:checked ~ section{
  perspective: 500px;
}


#cube:checked ~ section > ul{
  transform-style: preserve-3d;
}

#cube:checked ~ section figure{
  transform-origin: 250px 185px -250px;
  backface-visibility: hidden;
  transform: rotateY(-90deg);
  animation-name: cubeout;
  animation-duration: 1.5s;


}

#cube:checked ~ a:not(:target) + a:not(:target) + a:not(:target) +
a:not(:target) + a:not(:target) ~ section #shot1,
#cube:checked ~ a[name=picture1]:target ~ section #shot1,
#cube:checked ~ a[name=picture2]:target ~ section #shot2,
#cube:checked ~ a[name=picture3]:target ~ section #shot3,
#cube:checked ~ a[name=picture4]:target ~ section #shot4,
#cube:checked ~ a[name=picture5]:target ~ section #shot5{
  animation-name: cubein;
  animation-duration: 1.5s;
  transform: rotateY(0deg);
}
```

```
@keyframes cubein{
   0%   { transform: rotateY(90deg); }
   100% { transform: rotateY(0deg); }
}

@keyframes cubeout{
   0%   { transform: rotateY(0deg); }
   100% { transform: rotateY(-90deg); }
}

/* == [END] Cube == */
```

We set `perspective` and `transform-style` to the parent elements of those we want to transform. Then we define an origin that is centered on the `figure` elements but shifted 250 px away from the viewport.

Then we apply a rotating transformation around the y axis using the same mechanism as we did earlier with the `slidein` animation.

As a final touch, we tell the browser not to show the pictures when they're rotating opposite to the user's point of view. This is done with the `backface-visibility: hidden` statement.

A quick refresh in the browser and the result is as follows:

Chrome automatically disables 3D effects if the hardware of the PC running the browser doesn't have a GPU. To check if this behavior has been triggered, we can write about:GPU in the address bar.

Adding the slideshow mode

Now we're ready to implement the remaining two modes: slideshow and arrows. Let's begin with slideshow. All we have to do here is define an animation for each effect (**opacity**, **slidein**, and **cube**) and trigger it, paying attention to specifying a different delay (using the animation-delay property) to each figure element.

Let's begin with this last part and define a different delay for each figure element:

```
/* == [BEGIN] Animation == */

#animate:checked ~ section #shot1{
  animation-delay: 0s;
}

#animate:checked ~ section #shot2{
  animation-delay: 2.5s;
}

#animate:checked ~ section #shot3{
  animation-delay: 5s;
}

#animate:checked ~ section #shot4{
  animation-delay: 7.5s;
}

#animate:checked ~ section #shot5{
  animation-delay: 10s;
}

#animate:checked ~ section span{
  display: none;
}
```

If each animation lasts for 4 seconds (1.5 seconds to animate in, 1 second still, and 1.5 seconds to animate out), we need the second figure element to start after 2.5 seconds, exactly when the first one begins its exit animation. Later in this chapter, we'll learn how to make this CSS code adapt to a different number of images.

We can then repeat this step for the remaining `figure` elements and come out with the previous code.

The highlighted part is used to hide the bullets because they are not necessary during the slideshow.

Good! Now we have to write the animations. Let's start with the opacity animation:

```
/* opacity animation */
#opacity:checked ~ #animate:checked ~ section #shot1,
#opacity:checked ~ #animate:checked ~ section #shot2,
#opacity:checked ~ #animate:checked ~ section #shot3,
#opacity:checked ~ #animate:checked ~ section #shot4,
#opacity:checked ~ #animate:checked ~ section #shot5{
   opacity: 0;
   animation-name: opacity;
   animation-duration: 12.5s;
   animation-iteration-count: infinite;
}

@keyframes opacity{
   0%    { opacity: 0; }
   12%   { opacity: 1; }
   20%   { opacity: 1; }
   32%   { opacity: 0; }
   100%  { opacity: 0; }
}
```

We have to check that both the **opacity** and **animate** radio buttons are checked. Given this state, we can set the animation to `opacity` and choose a duration that is the value of the `animation-delay` property of the last `figure` element, `#shot5`, (10 seconds) plus its animation time (4 seconds) minus the time this animation overlaps the previous one (1.5 seconds).

Next we define some keyframes transforming the timing into a percentage (for example, 12% of 12.5 seconds = 1.5 seconds).

We can also easily extend this behavior for the two remaining animations, as follows:

- For the sliding effect, we start with the picture outside the visible area. Then we move it until it becomes completely visible. Lastly, after a while, we move it again out of the visible area, but from the other side.

```
/* slide animation */
#slidein:checked ~ #animate:checked ~ section #shot1,
#slidein:checked ~ #animate:checked ~ section #shot2,
#slidein:checked ~ #animate:checked ~ section #shot3,
#slidein:checked ~ #animate:checked ~ section #shot4,
```

```
#slidein:checked ~ #animate:checked ~ section #shot5{
  left: -500px;
  animation-name: slide;
  animation-duration: 12.5s;
  animation-iteration-count: infinite;
}


@keyframes slide{
  0%    { left: 500px; }
  12%   { left: 0px;   }
  20%   { left: 0px;   }
  32%  { left: -500px;}
  100%  { left: -500px;}
}
```

- For the rotating cube effect we basically do the same, but instead of using the
  left property we use the transform: rotate() one, and instead of sliding
  in the picture (-500 px, then 0 px, and finally 500 px) we rotate the cube (90
  degrees, then 0 degrees, and finally -90 degrees).

```
/* cube animation */
#cube:checked ~ #animate:checked ~ section #shot1,
#cube:checked ~ #animate:checked ~ section #shot2,
#cube:checked ~ #animate:checked ~ section #shot3,
#cube:checked ~ #animate:checked ~ section #shot4,
#cube:checked ~ #animate:checked ~ section #shot5{
  transform: rotateY(-90deg);
  transition: none;
  animation-name: cube;
  animation-duration: 12.5s;
  animation-iteration-count: infinite;
}


@keyframes cube{
  0%    { transform: rotateY(90deg);  }
  12%   { transform: rotateY(0deg);   }
  20%   { transform: rotateY(0deg);   }
  32%  { transform: rotateY(-90deg);}
  100%  { transform: rotateY(-90deg);}
}


/* == [END] Animation == */
```

Previous and next arrows

Ok, here comes the trickiest part: to create the arrows. What we are going to do in order to accomplish this task is:

1. Use CSS to transform each bullet into an arrow sign by changing its shape and using a nice background image.

2. Move all the arrows to the left of the picture, one above the other. In this way, the only visible arrow will be the one corresponding to the picture with the highest index.

3. Hide the arrow corresponding to the selected image.

4. Move all the arrows that follow the one corresponding to the selected image to the right, one above the other. In this way, on the left side there will remain only those arrows that correspond to the pictures with index lower than the selected one (for example, if we select picture number three, only the arrows of pictures number one and two will stay on the left, with the arrow of picture number two on the top of the stack).

5. Pick the arrow that follows the one corresponding to the selected image and change its z-index value in order to put it on top of the right stack.

The following is the corresponding CSS code:

```
/* == [BEGIN] Arrows == */

#arrows:checked ~ section span{
  position: static;
}


/* step 1 and 2: transform each bullet in an arrow sign and move all
the arrows to the left of the picture */
#arrows:checked ~ section a{
  display: block;
  width: 50px; height: 50px;
  background-image: url('../img/freccie.png');
  background-repeat: no-repeat;
  background-color: #000;
  background-position: -50px 0px;
  position: absolute;
  padding: 0;
  top: 50%;
  margin-top: -25px;
  margin-left: -70px;
  left: 0;
}
```

```
#arrows:checked ~ section a:hover{
  background-color: #333;
}


/* step 3: hide the arrow corresponding to the selected image */
#arrows:checked ~ a[name=picture1]:target ~ section
a[href="#picture1"],
#arrows:checked ~ a[name=picture2]:target ~ section
a[href="#picture2"],
#arrows:checked ~ a[name=picture3]:target ~ section
a[href="#picture3"],
#arrows:checked ~ a[name=picture4]:target ~ section
a[href="#picture4"],
#arrows:checked ~ a[name=picture5]:target ~ section
a[href="#picture5"]{
  display: none;
}


/* step 4: Move all the arrows that follow the one corresponding to
the selected image to the right, one above another */
#arrows:checked ~ a[name=picture1]:target ~ section
a[href="#picture1"] ~ a,
#arrows:checked ~ a[name=picture2]:target ~ section
a[href="#picture2"] ~ a,
#arrows:checked ~ a[name=picture3]:target ~ section
a[href="#picture3"] ~ a,
#arrows:checked ~ a[name=picture4]:target ~ section
a[href="#picture4"] ~ a,
#arrows:checked ~ a[name=picture5]:target ~ section
a[href="#picture5"] ~ a{
  display: block;
  position: absolute;
  margin-right: -70px;
  right: 0;
  left: auto;
}
/* step 5: Pick the arrow that follows the one corresponding to the
selected image and change its z-index in order to put it on top of the
right stack */
#arrows:checked ~ a[name=picture1]:target ~ section
a[href="#picture1"] + a,
#arrows:checked ~ a[name=picture2]:target ~ section
a[href="#picture2"] + a,
#arrows:checked ~ a[name=picture3]:target ~ section
a[href="#picture3"] + a,
```

```
#arrows:checked ~ a[name=picture4]:target ~ section
a[href="#picture4"] + a,
#arrows:checked ~ a[name=picture5]:target ~ section
a[href="#picture5"] + a{
  background-position: 0px 0px;
  z-index: 20;
}

/* == [END] Arrows == */
```

The following screenshot shows the result:

CSS preprocessors

In this section, we'll try to address the biggest issue with this project: the whole stylesheet is strictly dependent upon how many images are displayed in the gallery. Every effect is tailored around this number, and so adding a new image can cause a lot of work in our CSS.

To solve this problem we can use a **CSS preprocessor**, which lets us create a file in a language that includes some facilities such as loops and variables, and one that can be compiled into a CSS stylesheet.

We'll use Sass for this project. To install it, you need to first install Ruby (http://www.ruby-lang.sorg/en/downloads/) and then type `gem install sass` from a terminal emulator within your project directory (depending on your operating system, you may need to use `sudo gem install sass` instead).

Once this installation is complete, due to the fact that SCSS is a *superset* of CSS3, we can create an `scss/application.scss` file by duplicating the content of `css/application.css`.

Next we can prepend the whole code with a variable to contain the number of pictures our gallery currently holds:

```
/* == [BEGIN] Variables == */

$number_of_images: 5;

/* == [END] Variables == */

/* ... rest of CSS ... */
```

Now every time in the CSS we encounter a structure like the following one:

```
a[name=picture1]:target ~ section a[href="#picture1"],
a[name=picture2]:target ~ section a[href="#picture2"],
a[name=picture3]:target ~ section a[href="#picture3"],
a[name=picture4]:target ~ section a[href="#picture4"],
a[name=picture5]:target ~ section a[href="#picture5"]{
   background: #111;
}
```

We can change the code in a way that it generates the right number of selectors depending on `$number_of_images`:

```
@for $i from 1 through $number_of_images {
  a[name=picture#{$i}]:target ~ section a[href="#picture#{$i}"]{
    background: #111;
  }
}
```

Handling special cases

There are a few special cases, though, one of them is when we encounter a CSS selector that contains a string token repeated the number of times equal to the number of images. For example, the following line of CSS:

```
#opacity:checked ~ a:not(:target) + a:not(:target) + a:not(:target) +
a:not(:target) + a:not(:target) ~ section #shot1,
```

To transform the previous code into its variable-driven version, we have to create a function, a small piece of code that returns a string. We can write it just above the variable's declaration, as follows:

```
/* == [BEGIN] Function == */

@function negate-a-times($n) {
  $negate: unquote("");
  @for $i from 1 through $n - 1 {
    $negate: append($negate, unquote("a:not(:target) + "), space);
  }
    @return $negate + unquote("a:not(:target)")
}

/* == [END] Function == */
```

Now we can define a new variable that contains the string `a:not(:target)` repeated the number of times equal to the pictures in our gallery. So the new variable section in the `.scss` file will look like the following CSS snippet:

```
* == [BEGIN] Variables == */

$number_of_images: 5;
$negate_images: negate-a-times($number_of_images);

/* == [END] Variables == */
```

And finally, the previous CSS snippet can be transformed into:

```
#opacity:checked ~ #{$negate_images} ~ section #shot1,
```

Another thing we have to take care of is the timing of our animations. We have to dynamically calculate the total duration of the animation as well as the percentage of the three keyframes (enter animation, still, and exit animation) starting from the number of images in our gallery. To do so, we have to define a few extra variables just before the end of the `Variables` section of our `application.scss` file:

```
$animation_duration: 2.5 * $number_of_images;
$enter_animation: 0% + (1.5 / $animation_duration) * 100;
$still: 0% + (2.5 / $animation_duration) * 100;
```

```scss
$exit_animation: 0% + (4 / $animation_duration) * 100;
$animation_duration: $animation_duration + 0s;


/* == [END] Variables == */
```

In the previous few lines, we defined the total duration of the animation and then we converted the timings of the animation (1.5 seconds to animate in, 1 second still, and 1.5 seconds to animate out) into a percentage.

Last but not least, we have to run through our `.scss` code and transform each `animation-duration: 12.5s;` into `animation-duration: $animation_duration;`. We also have to change `@keyframes opacity`, `@keyframes slide`, and `@keyframes cube` as follows:

```scss
@keyframes opacity{
    0%      { opacity: 0; }
    #{$enter_animation}    { opacity: 1; }
    #{$still}              { opacity: 1; }
    #{$exit_animation}     { opacity: 0; }
    100%  { opacity: 0; }
}
@keyframes slide{
    0%      { left: 500px; }
    #{$enter_animation} { left: 0px; }
    #{$still}             { left: 0px; }
    #{$exit_animation}    { left: -500px; }
    100%  { left: -500px; }
}
@keyframes cube{
    0%      { transform: rotateY(90deg); }
    #{$enter_animation}    { transform: rotateY(0deg); }
    #{$still}               { transform: rotateY(0deg); }
    #{$exit_animation}     { transform: rotateY(-90deg); }
    100%  { transform: rotateY(-90deg); }
}
```

 The complete version of the `application.scss` file is available with the sources of the project.

To compile our `application.scss` file into `application.css`, we can invoke the following command using a terminal emulator from the root of the project:

```
sass scss/application.scss:css/application.css
```

By using these simple translating rules, we can transform our CSS into a very flexible SCSS. To prove it, we can try to remove a `figure` element from the HTML (with its corresponding a elements), change `$number_of_images:` to 4, recompile `application.scss`, and notice how the whole project keeps working smoothly.

Support for older browsers

Internet Explorer version 9 or below doesn't support CSS3 transition, nor CSS3 3D transforms, so this project can hardy be emulated on those browsers. We can however implement basic picture navigation while hiding all the other options. To achieve this, let's take advantage one more time of the conditional comments and substitute <html> with the following lines:

```
<!--[if lte IE 9]> <html class="lteie9"> <![endif]-->
<!--[if !IE]> --> <html> <!-- <![endif]-->
```

Next we need to add support for Internet Explorer 8 to some CSS3 selectors we used during the project. To do so, we have to add a library called Selectivizr (http://selectivizr.com/) that uses JavaScript to support most of the new CSS3 selectors. Selectivizr depends on jQuery, so we need to add it too. Lastly, we need to use a polyfill to make Internet Explorer 8 support the new HTML5 elements. The following is the snippet of code required to insert these three libraries, we need to add it just before the end of the head section in `index.html`:

```
<!--[if lte IE 8]>
<script src="http://html5shiv.googlecode.com/svn/trunk/html5.js"></
script>
<script src="https://ajax.googleapis.com/ajax/libs/jquery/1.8.3/
jquery.min.js"></script>
<script src="http://cdnjs.cloudflare.com/ajax/libs/selectivizr/1.0.2/
selectivizr-min.js"></script>
<![endif]-->
```

Finally, we can add a few CSS lines to hide everything except the first `figure` element when the `.lteie9` class is present. Additionally, we can take advantage of Sass in order to trigger `display:block` on the `figure` element corresponding to the selected bullet.

```
/* == [BEGIN] Old Browser == */

.lteie9 body > div > span,
.lteie9 body > div > input,
.lteie9 body > div > br,
.lteie9 body > div > label,
.lteie9 figure{
```

```
    display: none;
  }

  .lteie9 #{$negate_images} ~ section #shot1{
    display: block;
  }

  @for $i from 1 through $number_of_images {
    .lteie9 a[name=picture#{$i}]:target ~ section #shot#{$i}{
      display: block;
    }
  }

  /* == [END] Old Browser == */
```

Summary

CSS3 provides new, simplified methods to create stunning galleries without the use of JavaScript. Understandably, these techniques do not work with older non-CSS3-compliant browsers but we can detect these browsers and create fallback solutions.

In this chapter, we saw how we can create cool interaction mechanisms using only CSS3. Additionally, we discovered a nice way to generate CSS statically starting from a more flexible language.

Last but not least, we tried three cool animation effects. These can be easily mixed or new ones can be created by, for example, changing rotateX with rotateY, or left with top. In the next chapter, we'll explore how to obtain interesting parallax effects.

6
Parallax Scrolling

What is **parallax scrolling**? Parallax scrolling is a visual effect technique that tries to achieve a sense of depth by moving the elements of a scene, which have different speeds, for them to respond to a user action, such as the scrolling of a web page. This technique has been widely used in the 2D video game industry since the eighties.

In this chapter, we'll discover how to enhance our websites with parallax scrolling and other cool effects that respond to page scrolling. To achieve this, we'll dig into some advanced — and sometimes experimental — CSS 3D techniques and learn how to deal with perspective effectively.

Due to some implementation differences, we will then focus on how to obtain similar effects on different layout engines, such as WebKit and Gecko.

If you are working on a Windows operating system and using Chrome, you might have to switch to Firefox (or IE10) if the CSS 3D results are not as expected due to an absent or unsupported GPU. To check this, we can navigate to **about:gpu** from our Chrome browser and check whether the **3D CSS** checkbox has been enabled or not.

Here are the topics covered in this chapter:

- Discovering perspective
- Creating a cube
- Perspective origin
- CSS 3D parallax
- Differences between layout engines
- Changing parallax on page scroll
- Creating a parallax-enabled image gallery

Discovering perspective

As we started exploring in the previous chapter, CSS3 introduces the possibility to move our HTML elements in a three-dimensional space. We can now move and rotate them around each of the three axes, namely, x, y, and z. While dealing with movement around x and y axes is quite easy to figure out, things become a little messy when the z axis comes into play.

Moving an element along the z axis means getting it closer to or farther away from our viewpoint, but this action has some hidden problems, for example, take the following statement:

```
#element{
    transform: translateZ(100px);
}
```

How can we imagine moving an object of a distance measured in pixels towards us? To solve this dilemma, W3C has introduced a property called `perspective` that basically tells the browser what distance we're observing the page from.

So if we set `500px` as the perspective property, objects placed at the z axis with a distance of `250` pixels will look twice as big, and objects placed at the z axis with a distance of `500` pixels half as big.

Let's try this out with a small example:

```
<!doctype html>
<html>
<head>
  <meta charset="utf-8">
  <title>experimenting with perspective</title>

  <style>

  body{
    perspective: 500px;
    transform-style: 'preserve-3d';
  }

  #red-square{
    margin: auto;
    width: 500px;
    height: 500px;
    background: red;
    transform: rotateX(40deg);
  }
```

```
        </style>

        <script src="js/prefixfree.js"></script>

    </head>
    <body>

        <div id="red-square"></div>

    </body>
    </html>
```

If we run this code in a browser (such as Chrome, Firefox, or IE10) that supports CSS 3D features, we'll notice a result similar to the one shown in the following screenshot:

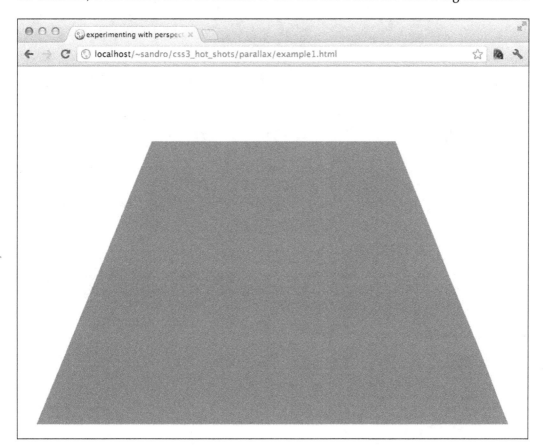

On increasing the `perspective` property's value, the result will look flatter, on the other hand, if this property is reduced, the red box will look stretched to the horizon. Here's an example with `perspective: 250px`:

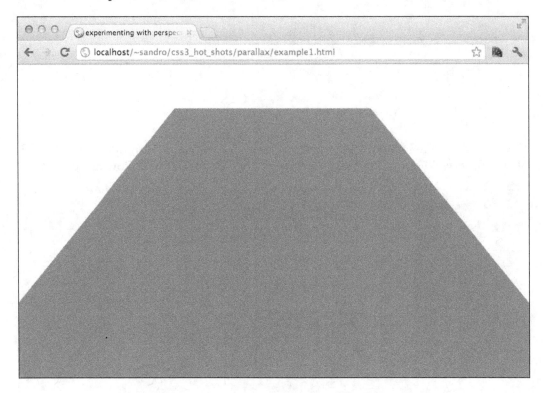

Creating a cube

To better understand some of the `perspective` properties, we can use what we have learned until now to create a real 3D cube using only CSS. We'll need six `div` tags, one for each side, plus one that will act as a container for the others:

```
<!doctype html>
<html>
  <head>
    <meta charset="utf-8">
    <title>A cube</title>

    <style>

    body, html{
      height: 100%;
      width: 100%;
```

```
    }

  </style>

  <script src="js/prefixfree.js"></script>
  </head>
  <body>
    <div id="container">
      <div class="square back"></div>
      <div class="square bottom"></div>
      <div class="square right"></div>
      <div class="square left"></div>
      <div class="square top"></div>
      <div class="square front"></div>
    </div>
  </body>
</html>
```

First of all, we have to apply some properties to the `#container` selector; let's insert the following chunk of CSS code within the `style` tag that we already defined:

```
#container{
  perspective: 500px;
  backface-visibility: visible;
  transform-style: 'preserve-3d';
  position: relative;
  height: 100%;
  width: 100%;
}
```

Here we tell the browser that what's inside this container must be rendered taking into account the position on the z axis, and we set the `perspective` property to `500px` for the `#container` selector and the elements within the container. Last but not least, we ask the browser to also render the rear face of the `div` tag that we'll use to create the cube.

Good, now let's create the faces. We can begin with some basic properties for `.square`:

```
.square{
  transform-style: 'preserve-3d';
  position: absolute;
  margin: -100px 0px 0px -100px;
  top: 50%;
  left: 50%;
  height: 200px;
  width: 200px;;
}
```

Okay, now each square lays down one over the other and we can begin adjusting them one by one. Let's start with .back, we have to move it away from the camera to half its size, so set the transform property to -100px:

```
.back{
  background: red;
  transform: translateZ(-100px);
}
```

Next we look at .left. Here we have to apply a rotation against its y axis first and then translate it by half of its size to the left-hand side. This is because every transformation, unless stated differently, has its origin in the center of the element; also, we have to remember that transformations are applied in sequence, so the element has to be translated against its z axis in order to achieve the correct result:

```
.left{
  background: blue;
  transform: rotateY(90deg) translateZ(-100px);
}
```

Here's a screenshot reminding us of the progress we have made so far:

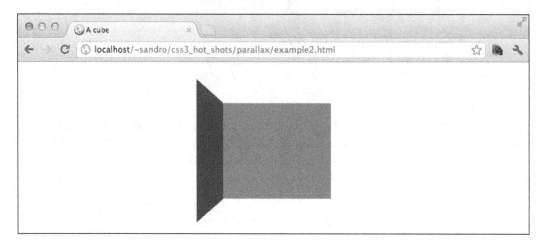

We can use the same strategy with all the remaining faces:

```
.right{
  background: yellow;
  transform: rotateY(-90deg) translateZ(-100px);
}

.front{
  background: green;
```

```
    transform: translateZ(100px);
}

.top{
  background: orange;
  transform: rotateX(-90deg) translateZ(-100px);
}

.bottom{
  background: purple;
  transform: rotateX(90deg) translateZ(-100px);
}
```

If we now try to take a screenshot of this experiment (as shown here), we may encounter a small disappointment:

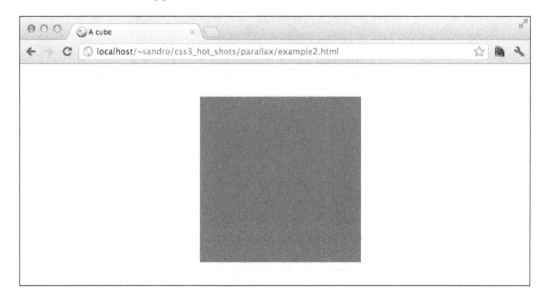

The `.front` selector's `div` tag covers all the other `div` tags. This small experiment shows us that the vanishing point of a scene is set, by default, to the center of the element that holds the `perspective` property.

The perspective-origin property

Luckily, we can easily change the vanishing point using the `perspective-origin` property that accepts two values, which can be expressed in all the common CSS measurement units or using literals, as happens with `background-position`.

So we'll add the following to `#container`:

```
perspective-origin: top left;
```

And obtain a result similar to the one shown here:

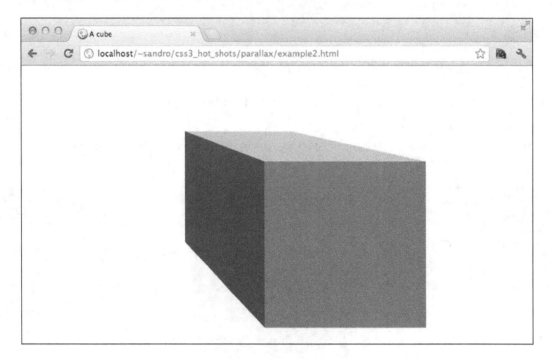

If we resize the browser window, we will also notice that the vanishing point changes because it is related to the `#container` selector that has the `width` and `height` properties set equal to the browser viewport.

This behavior is at the root of the trick that we'll use in the next chapter to build our parallax project.

CSS 3D parallax

Good, now we have the tools that we need to start building our project. The basic idea behind what we're going to create is that if we place elements at a different height and scroll while keeping the vanishing point in the center of the viewable area, then we can obtain a cool parallax scrolling effect.

As usual, we first need an HTML structure, so let's begin with this. Let's create the `index.html` file with the following code:

```
<!doctype html>
<html>
  <head>
  <meta charset="utf-8">
<link href='http://fonts.googleapis.com/css?family=Bowlby+One+SC'
rel='stylesheet' type='text/css' data-noprefix>
    <link rel="stylesheet" type="text/css" href="http://yui.yahooapis.
com/3.5.1/build/cssreset/cssreset-min.css" data-noprefix>
    <link rel="stylesheet" type="text/css" href="css/application.css">

    <script src="js/prefixfree.js"></script>
    <script src="https://ajax.googleapis.com/ajax/libs/jquery/1.7.2/
jquery.min.js"></script>

  </head>
  <body>

    <div id="body">
      <div id="container">


      </div>
    </div>

  </body>
</html>
```

Along with this page, we have to create a file named `css/application.css` that will hold our CSS properties and selectors. As we did in the previous example, we will stretch #body to fit the browser's viewport, so we can add a few lines of CSS code to `application.css`:

```
body,html{
  height: 100%;
}

#body{
  height: 100%;
  overflow-y: auto;
  overflow-x: hidden;
}
```

We've also added `overflow-y: auto` and `overflow-x: hidden` to the element, we'll discuss how these will be useful in a moment.

Implementing parallax scrolling in WebKit

Ok, before continuing we now have to focus on a single layout engine at a time; this is because there are some differences between WebKit and Firefox regarding the implementation of the CSS 3D properties, and so we have to handle the two cases separately. Let's start with WebKit.

We can take advantage of a neat class that Lea Verou's Prefix Free puts automatically on the `html` element of the page where it's inserted. This class has a name equal to the experimental prefix needed for the browser; so if we're viewing the page from Internet Explorer, the class is `-ms-`, and if from Firefox, it's `-moz-`.

So we can start adding the `perspective` and `transform-style` properties to `#body`, like we did in the previous example:

```
.-webkit- #body{
  perspective: 500px;
  transform-style: preserve-3d;
}
```

Now we have to deal with the `#container` selector; this has to be longer than the viewport—as usual all the images required for this project are located on the Packt Publishing website (`www.packtpub.com`):

```
#container{
  background-image: url('../img/grass.png');
  text-align: center;
  padding-bottom: 300px;
  /* to be removed when we'll have content */
min-height: 1000px;
}
```

Due to the fact that we've applied the `overflow` property to `#body`, the scroll bar that we'll see in the browser doesn't belong to the whole HTML document, but instead belongs to `#body`.

But `#body` also has a `perspective` property; this means that the vanishing point for the contained elements is always at the center of the browser screen, so we've achieved the structure that we wished to achieve at the beginning of this chapter.

To test our code, we can start adding a few elements inside the container and assign them different heights:

```
<div id="body">
  <div id="container">

  <!-- EXPERIMENT -->
```

```
    <img class="experiment1" src="img/pic1.jpg">
    <img class="experiment2" src="img/pic2.jpg">

  </div>
</div>
```

We can use `transform: translateZ();` to set up the height:

```
.experiment1{
  transform: translateZ(10px);
}

.experiment2{
  transform: translateZ(150px);
}
```

Good, now we can test what we've done so far in a WebKit-compliant browser:

While scrolling, we can note how the second image—the one closest to our viewpoint—moves faster than the first image. We've just achieved parallax on WebKit!

Implementing parallax scrolling in Gecko

There are some subtle implementation differences between Gecko and WebKit, along with some bugs.

First of all, the property `transform-style: preserve-3d` in Gecko doesn't propagate to all the descendants of the matched elements, but only to first-level children. The `perspective` and `perspective-origin` properties also do the same.

Fortunately, we can find a way around this problem. This can be done by expressing `perspective` as a transformation, for example:

```
transform: perspective(500px);
```

When we use this method, `perspective-origin` is no longer useful and `transform-origin` should be used in its place. Imposing `perspective` on Gecko-based browsers in this way results in the same behavior as when using perspective on WebKit-based browsers.

So we can add a few lines of CSS code using the same strategy we did with WebKit:

```
.-moz- #container{
  transform: perspective(500px);
  transform-style: preserve-3d;
}
```

If we open Firefox now and test our project, we'll see something like this:

Although the result looks like the one obtained with WebKit, scrolling the page in this case doesn't generate any parallax effect. After a quick analysis, we may be tempted to assume that this behavior is caused by having placed the `transform: perspective` property on the wrong element (`#container` instead of `#body`), but the truth is that we consciously chose to act this way due to a subtle bug (`https:// bugzilla.mozilla.org/show_bug.cgi?id=704469`) that removes the `transform: perspective` property from elements that have the `overflow` property.

So now the only way to make Gecko-based browsers behave as expected is to implement a small chunk of JavaScript that can dynamically modify our vanishing point, keeping it in the center of the browser window.

This script has to adjust the `transform-origin` property in response to the scrolling event:

```
<script>
  $(document).ready(function(){
    if($.browser.mozilla){
      $('#body').scroll(function(event){
        var viewport_height = $(window).height(),
          body_scrolltop = $('#body').scrollTop(),
          perspective_y = body_scrolltop + Math.round( viewport_height
/ 2 );

        $('#container').css({
          'transform-origin': 'center ' + perspective_y + "px",
          '-moz-transform-origin': 'center ' + perspective_y + "px",
        });
      })
    }
  });
</script>
```

Perfect! Now Gecko-based browsers will also behave as expected.

Implementing parallax scrolling in Internet Explorer

Internet Explorer 9 does not support CSS 3D transforms but IE10 does, so we can also try to run this project with that browser. To achieve the right behavior on IE10, we've to apply a few custom properties; this is because IE10 behaves in a way that is slightly different from those followed by the other two browsers.

Basically IE10 supports both the `perspective` and `transform: perspective` properties, but the former takes effect only on direct descendants of the element that have this property, and the latter works only on the element that has the property.

So we have to adopt a behavior closer to the one used for Gecko, but using `perspective` instead of `transform: perspective`. Here it is:

```
.-ms- #container{
  perspective: 500px;
}
```

Now we also need to change our JavaScript code a bit in order to affect `perspective-origin` when the browser is Internet Explorer and supports 3D transforms. Here's the code that can be used instead of the previous one:

```
// == for Firefox and MSIE users ==
$(document).ready(function(){
  if($.browser.mozilla || ( $.browser.msie&& Modernizr.csstransforms3d
)){
    $('#body').scroll(function(event){
      var viewport_height = $(window).height(),
        body_scrolltop = $('#body').scrollTop(),
        perspective_y = body_scrolltop + Math.round( viewport_height /
2 );

      if($.browser.mozilla){
        $('#container').css({
          'transform-origin': 'center ' + perspective_y + "px",
          '-moz-transform-origin': 'center ' + perspective_y + "px",
        });
      }else{
        $('#container').css({
          'perspective-origin': 'center ' + perspective_y + "px",
          '-ms-perspective-origin': 'center ' + perspective_y + "px",
        });
      }
    })
  }
});
```

To make this work, we must download Modernizr in order to check for CSS 3D support, we can create a custom build as we did in the previous chapter, but this time we only check the **CSS 3D Transforms** checkbox in the configuration panel (http://modernizr.com/download/). Next, we have to include the downloaded file (js/modernizr.js) in our page just after the other `script` tags:

```
<script src="js/modernizr.js"></script>
```

And here's a screenshot from IE10:

Adding some randomness to the gallery

Now that we've addressed the browser compatibility issues, we can safely remove the experimental comments and classes we previously attached to the images.

To create a sense of randomness, we can define a few groups of classes, each group having more variants of the same property, and then we can pick one class for each group of each image we want to display. Here's an example; let's add the following to `application.css`:

```css
/* sizes */
.size-a{
  width: 30%;
}

.size-b{
  width: 35%;
}
```

```
.size-c{
  width: 50%;
}

/* z-indexes */
.depth-a{
  transform: translateZ(10px);
  z-index: 1;
}

.depth-b{
  transform: translateZ(50px);
  z-index: 2;
}

.depth-c{
  transform: translateZ(100px);
  z-index: 3;
}

.depth-d{
  transform: translateZ(150px);
  z-index: 4;
}

.depth-e{
  transform: translateZ(200px);
  z-index: 5;
}
```

Now we can substitute the images used in the previous section with this list, where each image has a depth-* and one size-* attribute (where * denotes a randomly chosen class from the ones defined in the preceding code) attached to it:

```
<img class="basic_parallax depth-a size-a" src="img/picture1.jpg">
<img class="basic_parallax depth-b size-c" src="img/picture2.jpg">
<img class="basic_parallax depth-c size-b" src="img/picture3.jpg">
<img class="basic_parallax depth-b size-a" src="img/picture4.jpg">
<img class="basic_parallax depth-d size-c" src="img/picture5.jpg">
<img class="basic_parallax depth-e size-b" src="img/picture6.jpg">
<img class="basic_parallax depth-a size-c" src="img/picture7.jpg">
<img class="basic_parallax depth-c size-a" src="img/picture8.jpg">
<img class="basic_parallax depth-d size-c" src="img/picture9.jpg">
<img class="basic_parallax depth-a size-b" src="img/picture10.jpg">
<img class="basic_parallax depth-e size-b" src="img/picture11.jpg">
<img class="basic_parallax depth-a size-a" src="img/picture12.jpg">
<img class="basic_parallax depth-b size-c" src="img/picture13.jpg">
<img class="basic_parallax depth-c size-a" src="img/picture14.jpg">
```

Last but the least, let's define a basic CSS for each of these images:

```
img.basic_parallax{
  background: rgb(255,255,255);
  padding: 10px;
  box-shadow: 10px 10px10pxrgba(0,0,0,0.6);
  position: relative;
  margin: 10px;
}
```

Good, now let's reload our browser and test this out:

Rotating the images

Since we're dealing with a real 3D environment, we can try to develop more interesting effects using the same basic idea. For example, what if we rotate an element instead of simply moving it towards us? Let's try! First of all we need to add a few more images to our gallery; this time we also decided to add some decorative text, as follows:

```
<!-- DECKS -->
<img class="rotatextop" src="img/picture15.jpg">
<p>
   Keremma Dunes
   <small>Bretagne, Finist&eacute;re</small>
</p>
<img class="rotatexbottom" src="img/picture16.jpg">
<p class="depth-e">
   Rennes
   <small>Bretagne</small>
</p>
<img src="img/picture17.jpg">
```

Then we can use the `rotateX` transformation method on the images:

```
.rotatextop{
   transform-origin: top center;
   transform: rotateX(15deg);
}

.rotatexbottom{
   transform-origin: bottom center;
   transform: rotateX(-15deg);
}
```

A few more CSS properties to also style the paragraphs a little, and we're done:

```
p{
   text-align: center;
   font-family: 'Bowlby One SC', cursive;
   font-size: 6em;
   color: #e4ddc2;
}

p small{
   display: block;
   font-size: 0.4em;
   margin-top: -1em;
}
```

Here's a screenshot of the resulting gallery:

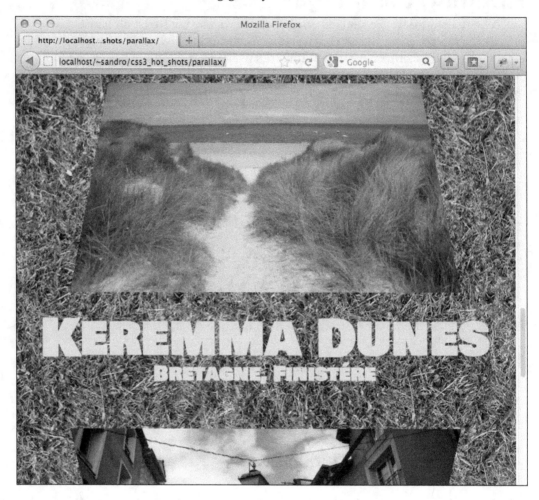

A 3D panorama

Let's also experiment with the rotateY method to complete this project. This time we'll use this property along with the perspective-origin property trick to create a cool panoramic effect.

First of all we need a panorama image, and then we can use an image editor to cut it into three pieces wherein the central image is roughly twice the size of the other two (for example, 800 x 800 px and 500 x 800 px). Once we've finished this, we can then add these images just before the end of the `#container` selector:

```
<p>
  Ortigia
  <small>Italy</small>
</p>
<img class="panorama left" src="img/panorama_left.jpg">
<img class="panorama center" src="img/panorama.jpg">
<img class="panorama right" src="img/panorama_right.jpg">
```

Now we can use the `rotateY` method for both `.left` and `.right`, as follows:

```
.panorama.left{
  transform-origin: center right;
  transform: rotateY(43deg);
}

.panorama.right{
  transform-origin: center left;
  transform: rotateY(-43deg);
}

.panorama.left, .panorama.right{
  width: 27%;
}

.panorama.center{
  width: 43.2%;
}
```

And here's the result:

Dealing with older browsers

Although the core effects of this project take advantage of some CSS 3D properties that cannot be emulated in older versions of the browser, the whole structure is made using only CSS 2-compatible properties and selectors, and so can be viewed from almost any browser:

Summary

Dealing with the third dimension could lead to a fight with a lot of small implementation differences, but once we tame them, the results are stunning and really enjoyable.

Here's what we have discussed in this chapter so far:

- CSS can be used to transform elements and move them in a 3D space
- We can use some properties to define the vanishing point in a 3D scene
- A cool parallax scrolling effect can be emulated by using CSS 3D properties
- Some JavaScript coding is required to deal with browser implementation differences

In the next chapter, we'll learn how to enhance the HTML5 `video` element with CSS.

7
Video Killed the Radio Star

Working with the CSS and HTML `video` element is, at the time of this writing, still sort of like practicing black magic. The main problem is that each browser leverages its particular video implementation technique; some of them use the GPU, while others use the same rendering engine used for the rest of the page. In this chapter, we'll explore how to create masks and effects on a running video by leveraging the power of SVG and CSS. Here's a list of the topics we'll cover:

- The HTML5 `video` element
- Masking with SVG
- SVG animations
- WebKit-specific masking properties
- CSS filters

The HTML5 video element

The HTML5 specification introduced new multimedia elements to allow a better integration of video and audio within a web page without the need to embed external plugins, such as Flash. Embedding a video is now as simple as writing this:

```
<video src="path/to/video">
```

There are a few caveats to consider, though; first of all, each browser supports only a fraction of the video codecs available, so if we want our element to be played, we need to encode our video at least in mp4 and webm and then use an alternative syntax to include both of these formats, as shown here:

```
<video>
  <source src="path/to/video.mp4" type="video/mp4">
  <source src="path/to/video.webm" type="video/webm">
</video>
```

Miro (http://www.mirovideoconverter.com/) is a good, free video converting software and works with both the Mac and Windows operating systems. It's really easy to use—just choose the desired output format and drop the file into the application window to begin the conversion process.

Once we set up our `video` element, we'll soon discover that most of the common CSS3 properties that should affect this element's shape don't behave the same way on all the browsers. For example, the `border-radius` property; in the following screenshot, this property is shown in action displaying videos in various browsers (note how this property behaves differently in different browsers):

WebKit-based browsers seem to ignore this property whereas Firefox and IE9 implement it correctly. This is probably due to the fact that Chrome and Safari play videos using the GPU and are thus less able to apply CSS modification on this content.

These differences between layout engines require a careful approach when dealing with video and CSS.

In the project, we're going to develop, using CSS, a small selection of modifications that can be applied to a video at runtime. Let's start with some basic masks.

Masks

Masks are useful tools when we need to hide part of some content; they are even more useful with videos because we can apply interesting effects that otherwise would require some dedicated software. There are several techniques we can employ to create a mask using HTML5/CSS3; however, support across browsers is inconsistent. In order to account for the inconsistencies, we will combine several techniques in our series.

To some small extent, we can use `border-radius` to mask our video, thus:

```
<!doctype html>
<html>

  <head>
    <meta charset="utf-8">
    <title>Masking</title>

    <style>
      video{
        border-radius: 300px;
      }
    </style>

  </head>

  <body>

    <video autoplay muted loop>
      <source src="video/sintel-trailer.mp4">
      <source src="video/sintel-trailer.webm">
    </video>

  </body>

</html>
```

As can you see, this method works with Firefox and IE, but for WebKit-based browsers we need to use a different approach.

If we're working using a web server (such as Apache or IIS), we may want to configure it to serve video files with the appropriate content type. To achieve this, we can create a .htaccess file in the root of our project (if we're using Apache) with the following content:

```
AddType video/ogg .ogv
AddType video/mp4 .mp4
AddType video/webm .webm
```

If we're using IIS, there is another procedure to be followed. This is fully explained in the guide at http://blog.j6consultants.com.au/2011/01/10/cross-browser-html5-video-running-under-iis-7-5/.

Since 2008, WebKit has supported a set of CSS properties that manage masks. We will use the webkit-mask-box-image selector to apply an image mask to our movie example. For this, we need a 300px black circle similar to the one in the following image:

And then, we will use the property introduced previously to set this black circle as the mask of the video element. When applied, the black parts of this image will let the underlying content be viewable whereas the white parts will keep the content completely hidden. Of course, gray colors can be used to partially hide/show the content.

```
video{
  border-radius: 300px;
  -webkit-mask-box-image: url(img/circle-mask.png) stretch;
}
```

And here's the result:

More advanced masking

For now, we can only afford to work with basic types of masking, that is everything that can be emulated with the `border-radius` property. But, if we simply try to create a mask with a small circle at its center, we discover that this combination is not feasible with the previous technique because a rounded corner can only lie on an element side. Luckily, we can switch to a more complex but powerful one, which involves the SVG format.

Both Gecko and WebKit support SVG masking via different CSS properties—Gecko-based browsers use the `mask` property, and WebKit uses `-webkit-mask-image`.

These properties don't just differ by name, they also behave differently:

- The `mask` property needs to be linked to an SVG element called `<mask>` that basically is a container for all the shapes we'll use to mask our `html` element

- The `-webkit-mask-image` property, on the other hand, needs to point to an SVG element containing all the shapes we want to overlay our video with

So, for example, here's how we can implement the `mask` property properly:

```
<!doctype html>
<html>

  <head>
    <meta charset="utf-8">
    <title>svg mask</title>

  </head>

  <body>

    <video autoplay muted loop>
      <source src="video/sintel-trailer.mp4">
      <source src="video/sintel-trailer.webm">
    </video>

    <style>
      video{
        mask: url('#circle');
      }
    </style>

    <svg>
      <defs>
        <mask id="circle">
          <circle cx="427" cy="240" r="100" fill="white"/>
        </mask>
      </defs>
    </svg>

  </body>

</html>
```

And here's how we can deal with the `-webkit-mask-image` property:

```
<!doctype html>
<html>

  <head>
    <meta charset="utf8">
    <title>svg mask</title>

  </head>

  <body>
```

```
<video autoplay muted loop>
  <source src="video/sintel-trailer.mp4">
  <source src="video/sintel-trailer.webm">
</video>

<style>
  video{
    -webkit-mask-image: url('svg/mask-circle.svg');
  }
</style>

</body>

</html>
```

Here, the SVG file, svg/mask-circle.svg, is defined as follows:

```
<?xml version="1.0" standalone="no"?>
<!DOCTYPE svg PUBLIC "-//W3C//DTD SVG 1.1//EN" "http://www.w3.org/
Graphics/SVG/1.1/DTD/svg11.dtd">

<svg version="1.1" xmlns="http://www.w3.org/2000/svg"
xmlns:xlink="http://www.w3.org/1999/xlink">
  <circle cx="427" cy="240" r="100" fill="white"/>
</svg>
```

In both these cases, the final result is the same and it's shown here:

The drawback of this method is that we have to create two distinct SVG fragments to suit both layout engines. Here comes a small improvement that can lead us to a better solution; by taking advantage of the `<use>` element, we can suit the needs of both properties in a single SVG file, named `svg/mask.svg`, as follows:

```
<?xml version="1.0" standalone="no"?>
<!DOCTYPE svg PUBLIC "-//W3C//DTD SVG 1.1//EN" "http://www.w3.org/
Graphics/SVG/1.1/DTD/svg11.dtd">

<svg version="1.1" xmlns="http://www.w3.org/2000/svg"
xmlns:xlink="http://www.w3.org/1999/xlink">
  <defs>
    <mask id="circle">
      <circle id="circle-element" cx="427" cy="240" r="100"
fill="white"/>
    </mask>
  </defs>
  <use xlink:href="#circle-element"/>
</svg>
```

By using this method, we can obtain the same result as the previous image on both browsers and with a single CSS statement:

```
<!doctype html>
<html>

  <head>
    <meta charset="utf-8">
    <title>svg mask</title>

    <style>
      video{
        mask: url('svg/mask.svg#circle');
        -webkit-mask-image: url('svg/mask.svg');
      }
    </style>

  </head>

  <body>

    <video autoplay muted loop>
      <source src="video/sintel-trailer.mp4">
      <source src="video/sintel-trailer.webm">
    </video>

  </body>

</html>
```

Well done! Now we're ready to implement some masks in our project.

Implementing the project

In this project, we'll use the beautiful trailer of Sintel (http://www.sintel.org/about/), a movie released under the Creative Commons license.

As usual, we'll need a basic project structure with some folders (css, img, svg, js, video). The videos used in this project are either available on the Sintel website or can be downloaded from Packt's website (www.packtpub.com) along with the completed project. We are also going to use **Prefix Free** (http://leaverou.github.com/prefixfree/), so let's download it and put it inside the js folder.

Let's create an index.html file to begin with:

```html
<!doctype html>
<html>

  <head>
    <meta charset="utf8">
    <title>Video killed the radio star</title>

    <link rel="stylesheet" type="text/css" href="http://yui.yahooapis.com/3.5.1/build/cssreset/cssreset-min.css" data-noprefix>
    <link rel="stylesheet" type="text/css" href="css/application.css">

    <script src="js/prefixfree.min.js"></script>

  </head>

  <body>

    <a id="mask" name="mask"></a>
    <a id="mask-stretch" name="mask-stretch"></a>
    <a id="mask-animate" name="mask-animate"></a>
    <a id="mask-animate-webkit" name="mask-animate-webkit"></a>
    <a id="mask-text" name="mask-text"></a>
    <a id="blur-filter" name="blur-filter"></a>
    <a id="grayscale-filter" name="grayscale-filter"></a>


    <video autoplay muted loop>
      <source src="video/sintel-trailer.mp4">
      <source src="video/sintel-trailer.webm">
    </video>

    <ul>
      <li>
        <a href="#">reset</a>
```

```
      </li>
      <li>
       <a href="#mask">mask</a>
      </li>
      <li>
        <a href="#mask-animate">animated mask</a>
      </li>
      <li>
        <a href="#mask-animate-webkit">animated mask (webkit)</a>
      </li>
      <li>
        <a href="#mask-text">text mask</a>
      </li>
      <li>
        <a href="#blur-filter">blur filter</a>
      </li>
      <li>
        <a href="#grayscale-filter">grayscale filter</a>
      </li>
    </ul>
  </body>

</html>
```

Then, in `application.css`, let's do some basic CSS styling as well as the masking techniques that we just introduced:

```
html{
  min-height: 100%;
  background-image: linear-gradient(top, black, black 500px, white);
  background-size: cover;
  background-repeat: no-repeat;
}

video{
  display: block;
  margin: 0 auto;
}

ul{
  text-align: center;
  position: absolute;
  bottom : 100px;
  width: 100%;
}

li{
```

```
    display: inline;
}

li > a{
  display: inline-block;
  padding: 5px;
  background: #FFF;
  border: 3px solid black;
  text-decoration: none;
  font-family: sans-serif;
  color: black;
  font-size: 10px;
}


/* ==[BEGIN] Masking == */

a[name="mask"]:target ~ video{
  mask: url('../svg/mask.svg#circle');
  -webkit-mask-image: url('../svg/mask.svg');
}
```

And here's the result once the **mask** button is pressed:

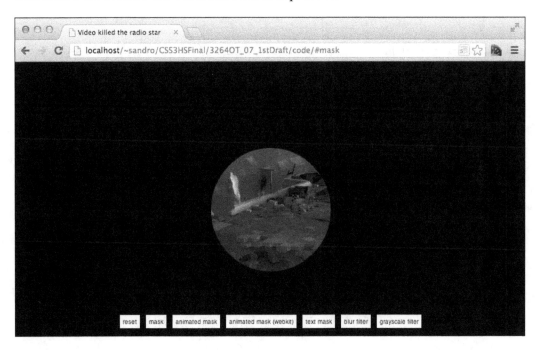

Animating masks

SVG supports animations via some special elements. In this chapter, we'll use the most generic one, `<animate>`.

Here's an example:

```
<circle ... >
<animate attributeType="CSS" attributeName="opacity" from="1" to="0"
dur="5s" repeatCount="indefinite" />
</circle>
```

The element that contains `<animate>` gets its property animated as described by the options specified within the tag's attributes. In the preceding code, we ask the browser to animate the opacity of the circle from being completely visible to getting hidden in five seconds.

So, we'll be able to obtain an animation that works both on Gecko and WebKit browsers if we create a new SVG file, named `svg/mask-animate.svg`, with the following code:

```
<?xml version="1.0" standalone="no"?>
<!DOCTYPE svg PUBLIC "-//W3C//DTD SVG 1.1//EN" "http://www.w3.org/
Graphics/SVG/1.1/DTD/svg11.dtd">

<svg version="1.1" xmlns="http://www.w3.org/2000/svg"
xmlns:xlink="http://www.w3.org/1999/xlink">
  <defs>
    <mask id="circle">
      <circle id="circle-element" cx="427" cy="240" r="100"
fill="white">
        <animate attributeName="r" values="100;200;100" dur="5s"
repeatCount="indefinite" />
      </circle>
    </mask>
  </defs>
  <use xlink:href="#circle-element"/>
</svg>
```

Here's the CSS we need to add to `css/application.css`:

```
a[name="mask-animate"]:target ~ video{
  mask: url('../svg/mask-animate.svg#circle');
  -webkit-mask-image: url('../svg/mask-animate.svg');
}
```

And here's the result with the mask that grows and shrinks in a 5-second animation:

WebKit-specific properties

There are some extra properties related to masking that are available only for WebKit browsers; these work exactly as their background property counterparts, so here's the list, taken from the original WebKit blog post:

- -webkit-mask (background): This is a shortcut for all the other properties

- -webkit-mask-attachment (background-attachment): This defines whether the mask should scroll within the content or not

- -webkit-mask-clip (background-clip): This specifies the clipping area of the mask

- `-webkit-mask-position` (`background-position`): This property specifies the position of the mask within the element

- `-webkit-mask-origin` (`background-origin`): This specifies where the coordinates 0,0 should be placed within the element (for example, at the beginning of the padding area using `padding-box` as the value)

- `-webkit-mask-image` (`background-image`): This points to one or more images or gradients to be used as masks

- `-webkit-mask-repeat` (`background-repeat`): This defines whether the mask should be repeated or not and and also whether in one or both directions

- `-webkit-mask-composite` (`background-composite`): This specifies how two masks should merge when overlapping with each other

- `-webkit-mask-box-image` (`border-image`): This points to one or more images or gradients to be used as masks with the same properties and behavior used to define border images

With these new properties, we can create some extra effects by taking advantage of CSS transitions, for example, we can mask our movie with a gradient and then, using `:hover`, change its mask position; here's the CSS code:

```
a[name="mask-animate-webkit"]:target ~ video{
  -webkit-mask-position: 0 100%;
  -webkit-mask-size: 100% 200%;
  -webkit-mask-image: -webkit-gradient(linear, center top, center
bottom,
      color-stop(0.00,  rgba(0,0,0,1)),
      color-stop(1.00,  rgba(0,0,0,0))
    );
  -webkit-transition: -webkit-mask-position 1s;
}

a[name="mask-animate-webkit"]:target ~ video:hover{
  -webkit-mask-position: 0 0;
}
```

Due to the fact that these WebKit-mask properties were created during 2008 and were probably never updated since then, we have to use the old WebKit gradient syntax; apart from that, everything else is pretty straightforward, as shown is the following image:

Masking with text

We can use text to mask a `video` element; the procedure is similar to what we saw previously, but of course, we need to craft another ad hoc SVG file, named `svg/mask-text.svg`:

```
<?xml version="1.0" standalone="no"?>
<!DOCTYPE svg PUBLIC "-//W3C//DTD SVG 1.1//EN" "http://www.w3.org/
Graphics/SVG/1.1/DTD/svg11.dtd">

<svg xmlns="http://www.w3.org/2000/svg" xmlns:xlink="http://www.
w3.org/1999/xlink" width="1000" height="280" version="1.1">
  <defs>
    <mask id="sintel-mask">
      <text x="0" y="300" id="sintel" fill="white" style="color:
black;font-size:210px;
```

```
       font-family: Blue Highway, Arial Black, sans-serif;">SINTEL</text>
         </mask>
      </defs>
      <text x="0" y="80%" id="sintel" fill="white" style="color:
   black;font-size:240px;
         font-family: Blue Highway, Arial Black, sans-serif;">SINTEL</text>
   </svg>
```

Here, we cannot take advantage of the `<use>` element because of another difference between how mask positioning and mask size are determined.

Gecko-based browsers can only afford fixed coordinates, while WebKit-based browsers can stretch the mask to fit the screen, if instead of `-webkit-mask-image`, we use `-webkit-mask-box-image` (as we saw in the very first example in this chapter).

Here's the required CSS:

```
   a[name="mask-text"]:target ~ video{
      mask: url('../svg/mask-text.svg#sintel-mask');
      -webkit-mask-box-image: url('../svg/mask-text.svg');
   }
```

And here's a screenshot of the result:

Filters

Along with masks, filters are other powerful modifiers that can be applied to elements in order to obtain various effects, such as blur, grayscale, and many more. Of course, there are drawbacks; at the time of writing, filters support is inhomogeneous. The following are some of the drawbacks:

- IE9 supports some effects using the well-known `progid` filters
- Firefox supports filters if declared within an SVG fragment
- Chrome, Safari, and other WebKit-based browsers support the last CSS filter specification
- IE10 has not yet confirmed support for these properties, plus it will drop support for `progid` filters

So, let's implement the blur filter trying to keep the support as wide as possible. First, we'll handle WebKit, which is very easy:

```
-webkit-filter: blur(3px);
```

The parameter passed to the `blur` function is the pixel radius of the effect. Next comes Gecko support; for this we have to use the `feGaussianBlur` element within a properly done SVG file, named `svg/filters.svg`:

```
<?xml version="1.0" standalone="no"?>
<!DOCTYPE svg PUBLIC "-//W3C//DTD SVG 1.1//EN" "http://www.w3.org/
Graphics/SVG/1.1/DTD/svg11.dtd">
<svg xmlns="http://www.w3.org/2000/svg" xmlns:xlink="http://www.
w3.org/1999/xlink" version="1.1">
  <defs>
    <filter id="blur">
    <feGaussianBlur stdDeviation="3" />
  </filter>
  </defs>
</svg>
```

And then, we can refer to this effect using the `filter` property supported by Gecko:

```
filter: url('../svg/filters.svg#blur');
```

Next, we can also implement this effect on IE9 by using the `progid` filters:

```
filter:progid:DXImageTransform.Microsoft.Blur(pixelradius=3);
```

Here's the final CSS. Note how we added a `:hover` selector trick to change the blur on mouseover; this actually works only on WebKit-based browsers, but the support can easily be extended by following the previously-stated rules:

```
a[name="blur-filter"]:target ~ video{
  -webkit-filter: blur(3px);
  -webkit-transition: -webkit-filter 1s;
  filter: url('../svg/filters.svg#blur');
}

.-ms- a[name="blur-filter"]:target ~ video{
  filter:progid:DXImageTransform.Microsoft.Blur(pixelradius=3);
}

a[name="blur-filter"]:target ~ video:hover{
  -webkit-filter: blur(0px);
}
```

We also have to deal with the fact that both Gecko and IE9 refer to the same `filter` property but with really different valorizations. To find a way around this problem, we can use the special `-ms-` class added by Lea Verou's prefixfree library on the top-level `html` element.

And here's the result:

On the current stable Chrome version, the `filter` property seems as if it is not working out of the box. This is because we need to enable filters on accelerated elements. So let's open a new tab and type `about:flags` into the address bar and enable the **GPU Accelerated SVG and CSS Filters** experimental feature.

Grayscale filter

Let's look at one more filter, grayscale! A grayscale filter basically turns all the colors of the target image or video to a corresponding gray value.

Here's the complete CSS:

```
/* == [BEGIN] Grayscale filter == */

a[name="grayscale-filter"]:target ~ video{
  -webkit-filter: grayscale(1);
  filter: url('../svg/filters.svg#grayscale');
}

.-ms- a[name="grayscale-filter"]:target ~ video{
  filter:progid:DXImageTransform.Microsoft.BasicImage(grayscale=1);
}
```

And here's the SVG snippet:

```
<filter id="grayscale">
        <feColorMatrix values="0.3333 0.3333 0.3333 0 0
                               0.3333 0.3333 0.3333 0 0
                               0.3333 0.3333 0.3333 0 0
                               0      0      0      1 0"/>
</filter>
```

And finally, here's a screenshot taken from IE9:

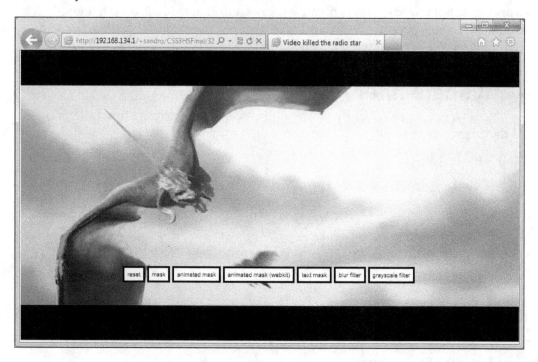

There are many more filters that can be applied to our elements; for a complete list, we can have a look at:

- The official filter draft specifications at
  `https://dvcs.w3.org/hg/FXTF/raw-file/tip/filters/index.html`

- The **Filter Effects** section of the SVG specifications at
  `http://www.w3.org/TR/SVG/filters.html`

- The **Filters** section on MSDN at
  `http://msdn.microsoft.com/en-us/library/ms532847(v=vs.85).aspx`

Summary

In this chapter, we discovered how to deal with HTML5 `video` elements using CSS; we learned that browsers behave very differently, and therefore we have to implement various techniques to achieve compatibility.

We figured out how to dynamically add masks — static or animated — and how to create a filter, either using SVG or the new W3C specifications.

In the next chapter we'll learn how to deal with complex animations.

8
Go Go Gauges

In web application development, gauges can be useful for showing complicated or dynamic data in a visual or intuitive way. In this chapter, we'll learn how to create a fully customizable animated gauge that can respond to real-time changes. We'll also discuss techniques to port this type of widget for support in older web browsers. We'll start by learning about a cool SASS enhancement called **Compass**; this is another way to deal with CSS3 experimental prefixes. The following is the list of the topics we'll discuss:

- A basic gauge structure
- Using Compass
- Using rem
- Moving the arrow
- Animating the arrow
- Dealing with older browsers

A basic gauge structure

Let's begin with a new project; as usual we need to create an `index.html` file. This time the markup involved is so small and compact that we can add it right now:

```html
<!doctype html>
<html>
<head>
<meta charset="utf-8">
<meta http-equiv="X-UA-Compatible" content="IE=edge" />

  <title>Go Go Gauges</title>
```

```
    <link rel="stylesheet" type="text/css" href="css/application.css">
  </head>
  <body>

    <div data-gauge data-min="0" data-max="100" data-percent="50">
      <div data-arrow></div>
    </div>

  </body>
  </html>
```

The gauge widget is identified by the data-gauge attribute and defined with three other custom data attributes; namely, data-min, data-max, and data-percent, which indicate the respective minimum and maximum value of the range and the current arrow position expressed in percentage value.

Within the element marked with the data-gauge attribute, we have defined a div tag that will become the arrow of the gauge.

To start with the styling phase, we first need to equip ourselves with a framework that is easy to use and can give us the opportunity to generate CSS code. We decide to go for SASS, the same as we used in *Chapter 5*, *An Image Gallery*, so we first need to install Ruby (http://www.ruby-lang.org/en/downloads/) and then enter the following from a command-line terminal:

```
gem install sass
```

 You would probably need to execute the following command if you are working in Unix/Linux environments:
```
sudo gem install sass
```

Installing Compass

For this project we'll also use Compass, a SASS extension able to add some interesting features to our SASS stylesheet.

To install Compass, we have to just enter gem install compass (or sudo gem install compass) in a terminal window. After the installation procedure is over, we have to create a small config.rb file in the root folder of our project using the following code:

```
# Require any additional compass plugins here.

# Set this to the root of your project when deployed:
http_path = YOUR-HTTP-PROJECT-PATH
css_dir = "css"
```

```
sass_dir = "scss"
images_dir = "img"
javascripts_dir = "js"

# You can select your preferred output style here (can be overridden
via the command line):
# output_style = :expanded or :nested or :compact or :compressed

# To enable relative paths to assets via compass helper functions.
Uncomment:
relative_assets = true

# To disable debugging comments that display the original location of
your selectors. Uncomment:
# line_comments = false


preferred_syntax = :sass
```

The `config.rb` file helps Compass to understand the location of the various assets of the project; let's have a look at these options in detail:

- `http_path`: This must be set to the HTTP URL related to the project's root folder

- `css_dir`: This contains the relative path to the folder where the generated CSS files should be saved

- `sass_dir`: This contains the relative path to the folder that contains our `.scss` files

- `images_dir`: This contains the relative path to the folder that holds all the images of the project

- `javascripts_dir`: This is similar to `images_dir`, but for JavaScript files

There are other options available; we can decide whether the output CSS should be compressed or not, or we can ask Compass to use relative paths instead of absolute ones. For a complete list of all the options available, see the documentation at `http://compass-style.org/help/tutorials/configuration-reference/`.

Next, we can create the folder structure we just described, providing our project with the css, img, js, and scss folders. Lastly, we can create an empty scss/ `application.scss` file and start discovering the beauty of Compass.

CSS reset and vendor prefixes

We can ask Compass to regenerate the CSS file after each update to its SCSS counterpart. To do so, we need to execute the following command from the root of our project using a terminal:

```
compass watch .
```

Compass provides an alternative to the Yahoo! reset stylesheet we used in our previous project. To include this stylesheet, all we have to do is add a SASS include directive to our `application.scss` file:

```
@import "compass/reset";
```

If we check `css/application.css`, the following is the result (trimmed):

```
/* line 17, ../../../../.rvm/gems/ruby-1.9.3-p194/gems/compass-0.12.2/
frameworks/compass/stylesheets/compass/reset/_utilities.scss */
html, body, div, span, applet, object, iframe,
h1, h2, h3, h4, h5, h6, p, blockquote, pre,
a, abbr, acronym, address, big, cite, code,
del, dfn, em, img, ins, kbd, q, s, samp,
small, strike, strong, sub, sup, tt, var,
b, u, i, center,
dl, dt, dd, ol, ul, li,
fieldset, form, label, legend,
table, caption, tbody, tfoot, thead, tr, th, td,
article, aside, canvas, details, embed,
figure, figcaption, footer, header, hgroup,
menu, nav, output, ruby, section, summary,
time, mark, audio, video {
  margin: 0;
  padding: 0;
  border: 0;
  font: inherit;
  font-size: 100%;
  vertical-align: baseline;
}

/* line 22, ../../../../.rvm/gems/ruby-1.9.3-p194/gems/compass-0.12.2/
frameworks/compass/stylesheets/compass/reset/_utilities.scss */
html {
  line-height: 1;
}

...
```

Notice also how the generated CSS keeps a reference to the original SCSS; this comes in handy when it's a matter of debugging some unexpected behaviors in our page.

The next @import directive will take care of the CSS3 experimental vendor prefixes. By adding @import "compass/css3" on top of the application.scss file, we ask Compass to provide us with a lot of powerful methods for adding experimental prefixes automatically; for example, the following snippet:

```
.round {
    @include border-radius(4px);
}
```

Is compiled into the following:

```
.round {
    -moz-border-radius: 4px;
    -webkit-border-radius: 4px;
    -o-border-radius: 4px;
    -ms-border-radius: 4px;
    -khtml-border-radius: 4px;
    border-radius: 4px;
}
```

Equipped with this new knowledge, we can now start deploying the project.

Using rem

For this project we want to introduce rem, a measurement unit that is almost equivalent to em, but is always relative to the root element of the page. So, basically we can define a font size on the html element and then all the sizes will be related to it:

```
html{
    font-size: 20px;
}
```

Now, 1rem corresponds to 20px; the problem of this measurement is that some browsers, such as Internet Explorer version 8 or less, don't actually support it. To find a way around this problem, we can use the following two different fallback measurement units:

- em: The good news is that em, if perfectly tuned, works exactly as rem; the bad news is that this measurement unit is relative to the element's font-size property and is not relative to html. So, if we decide to pursue this method, we then have to take extra care every time we deal with font-size.

- px: We can use a fixed unit pixel size. The downside of this choice is that in older browsers, we're complicating the ability to dynamically change the proportions of our widget.

In this project, we will use pixels as our unit of measurement. The reason we have decided this is because one of the rem benefits is that we can change the size of the gauge easily by changing the font-size property with media queries. This is only possible where media queries and rem are supported.

Now, we have to find a way to address most of the duplication that would emerge from having to insert every statement containing a space measurement unit twice (rem and px). We can easily solve this problem by creating a SASS mixin within our application.scss file as follows (for more info on SASS mixins, we can refer to the specifications page at http://sass-lang.com/docs/yardoc/file.SASS_REFERENCE.html#mixins):

```
@mixin px_and_rem($property, $value, $mux){
    #{$property}: 0px + ($value * $mux);
    #{$property}: 0rem + $value;
}
```

So the next time instead of writing the following:

```
#my_style{
width: 10rem;
}
```

We can instead write:

```
#my_style{
@include px_and_rem(width, 10, 20);
}
```

In addition to that, we can also save the multiplier coefficient between px and rem in a variable and use it in every call to this function and within the html declaration; let's also add this to application.scss:

```
$multiplier: 20px;

html{
    font-size: $multiplier;
}
```

Of course, there are still some cases in which the @mixin directive that we just created doesn't work, and in such situations we'll have to handle this duality manually.

Basic structure of a gauge

Now we're ready to develop at least the basic structure of our gauge, which includes the rounded borders and the minimum and maximum range labels. The following code is what we need to add to `application.scss`:

```scss
div[data-gauge]{
  position: absolute;

  /* width, height and rounded corners */
  @include px_and_rem(width, 10, $multiplier);
  @include px_and_rem(height, 5, $multiplier);
  @include px_and_rem(border-top-left-radius, 5, $multiplier);
  @include px_and_rem(border-top-right-radius, 5, $multiplier);

  /* centering */
  @include px_and_rem(margin-top, -2.5, $multiplier);
  @include px_and_rem(margin-left, -5,  $multiplier);
  top: 50%;
  left: 50%;

  /* inset shadows, both in px and rem */
box-shadow: 0 0 #{0.1 * $multiplier} rgba(99,99,99,0.8), 0 0 #{0.1 *
$multiplier} rgba(99,99,99,0.8) inset;
  box-shadow: 0 0 0.1rem rgba(99,99,99,0.8), 0 0 0.1rem
rgba(99,99,99,0.8) inset;

  /* border, font size, family and color */
  border: #{0.05 * $multiplier} solid rgb(99,99,99);
  border: 0.05rem solid rgb(99,99,99);

  color: rgb(33,33,33);
  @include px_and_rem(font-size, 0.7, $multiplier);
  font-family: verdana, arial, sans-serif;

  /* min label */
  &:before{
    content: attr(data-min);
    position: absolute;
    @include px_and_rem(bottom, 0.2, $multiplier);
    @include px_and_rem(left, 0.4, $multiplier);
  }

  /* max label */
  &:after{
    content: attr(data-max);
    position: absolute;
    @include px_and_rem(bottom, 0.2, $multiplier);
    @include px_and_rem(right, 0.4, $multiplier);
  }
}
```

With `box-shadow` and `border`, we can't use the `px_and_rem` mixin, so we duplicated these properties using `px` first and then `rem`.

The following screenshot shows the result:

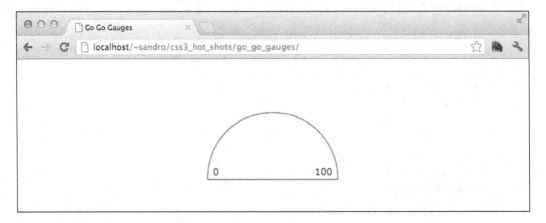

Gauge tick marks

How to handle tick marks? One method would be by using images, but another interesting alternative is to benefit from multiple background support and create those tick marks out of gradients. For example, to create a vertical mark, we can use the following within the `div[data-gauge]` selector:

```
linear-gradient(0deg, transparent 46%, rgba(99, 99, 99, 0.5) 47%,
rgba(99, 99, 99, 0.5) 53%, transparent 54%)
```

Basically, we define a very small gradient between transparent and another color in order to obtain the tick mark. That's the first step, but we're yet to deal with the fact that each tick mark must be defined with a different angle. We can solve this problem by introducing a SASS function that takes the number of tick marks to print and iterates up to that number while also adjusting the angles of each mark. Of course, we also have to take care of experimental vendor prefixes, but we can count on Compass for that.

The following is the function. We can create a new file called `scss/_gauge.scss` for this and other gauge-related functions; the leading underscore is to tell SASS to not create a `.css` file out of this `.scss` file, because it will be included in a separate file.

```
@function gauge-tick-marks($n, $rest){
  $linear: null;
  @for $i from 1 through $n {
    $p: -90deg + 180 / ($n+1) * $i;
```

```
    $linear: append($linear, linear-gradient( $p, transparent 46%,
  rgba(99,99,99,0.5) 47%, rgba(99,99,99,0.5) 53%, transparent 54%),
  comma);
  }
  @return append($linear, $rest);
}
```

We start with an empty string adding the result of calling the `linear-gradient` Compass function, which handles experimental vendor prefixes, with an angle that varies based on the current tick mark index.

To test this function out, we first need to include `_gauge.scss` in `application.scss`:

```
@import "gauge.scss";
```

Next, we can insert the function call within the `div[data-gauge]` selector in `application.scss`, specifying the number of tick marks required:

```
@include background(gauge-tick-marks(11,null));
```

The `background` function is also provided by Compass and it is just another mechanism to deal with experimental prefixes. Unfortunately, if we reload the projects the results are far from expected:

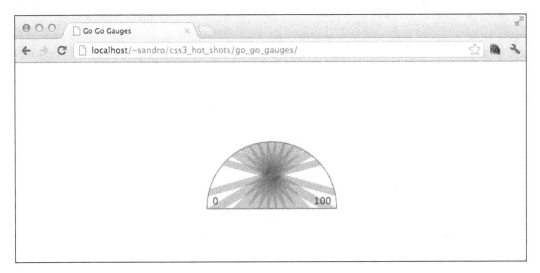

Although we can see a total of 11 stripes, they are of the wrong sizes and in the wrong position. To resolve this, we will create some functions to set the correct values for `background-size` and `background-position`.

Dealing with background size and position

Let's start with `background-size`, the easiest. Since we want each of the tick marks to be exactly `1rem` in size, we can proceed by creating a function that prints **1rem 1rem** as many times as the number of the passed parameter; so let's add the following code to `_gauge.scss`:

```
@function gauge-tick-marks-size($n, $rest){
  $sizes: null;
  @for $i from 1 through $n {
    $sizes: append($sizes, 1rem 1rem, comma);
  }
  @return append($sizes, $rest, comma);
}
```

We already noticed the `append` function; an interesting thing to know about it is that the last parameter of this function lets us decide if some letter must be used to concatenate the strings being created. One of the available options is `comma`, which perfectly suits our needs.

Now, we can add a call to this function within the `div[data-gauge]` selector:

```
background-size: gauge-tick-marks-size(11, null);
```

And the following is the result:

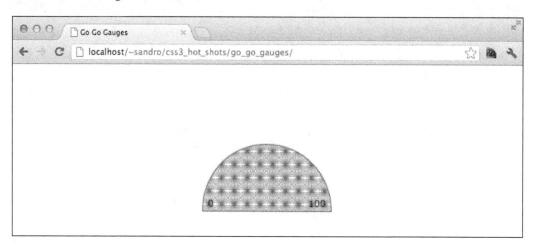

Now the tick marks are of the right size, but they are displayed one above the other and are repeated all across the element. To avoid this behavior, we can simply add `background-repeat: no-repeat` just below the previous instruction:

```
background-repeat: no-repeat;
```

On the other hand, to handle the position of the tick marks we need another SASS function; this time it's a little more complex and involves a bit of trigonometry. Each gradient must be placed in the function of its angle—x is the cosine of that angle and y the sine. The `sin` and `cos` functions are provided by Compass, we need just to handle the shift, because they are referred to the center of the circle whereas our css property's origin is in the upper-left corner:

```
@function gauge-tick-marks-position($n, $rest){
  $positions: null;
  @for $i from 1 through $n {
    $angle: 0deg + 180 / ($n+1) * $i;
    $px: 100% * ( cos($angle) / 2 + 0.5 );
    $py: 100% * (1 - sin($angle));
    $positions: append($positions, $px $py, comma);
  }
  @return append($positions, $rest, comma);
}
```

Now we can go ahead and add a new line inside the `div[data-gauge]` selector:

```
background-position: gauge-tick-marks-position(11, null);
```

And here's the much-awaited result:

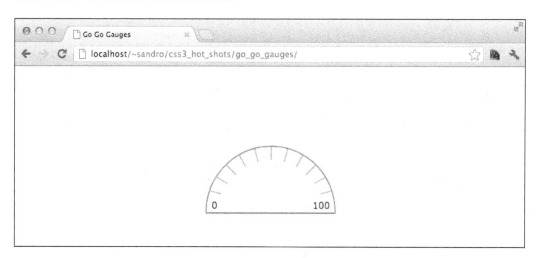

The next step is to create a `@mixin` directive to hold these three functions together, so we can add the following to `_gauge.scss`:

```
@mixin gauge-background($ticks, $rest_gradient, $rest_size, $rest_
position) {
```

```
    @include background-image(
      gauge-tick-marks($ticks, $rest_gradient)
    );


    background-size: gauge-tick-marks-size($ticks, $rest_size);
    background-position: gauge-tick-marks-position($ticks,
  $rest_position);
    background-repeat: no-repeat;
  }
```

And replace what we placed inside div[data-gauge] in this chapter with a
single invocation:

```
  @include gauge-background(11, null, null, null );
```

We've also left three additional parameters to define extra values for background,
background-size, and background-position, so we can, for example, easily add a
gradient background:

```
  @include gauge-background(11,
    radial-gradient(50% 100%, circle, rgb(255,255,255),
  rgb(230,230,230)),
    cover,
    center center
  );
```

And following is the screenshot:

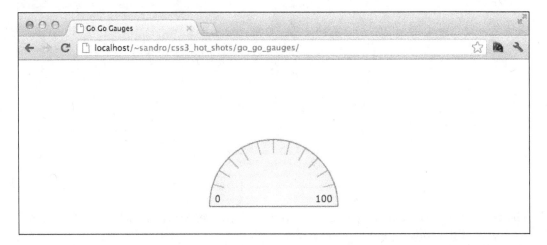

Creating the arrow

To create an arrow we can start by defining the circular element in the center of the gauge that holds the arrow. This is easy and doesn't introduce anything really new; here's the code that needs to be nested within the `div[data-gauge]` selector:

```
div[data-arrow]{
    position: absolute;
    @include px_and_rem(width, 2, $multiplier);
    @include px_and_rem(height, 2, $multiplier);
    @include px_and_rem(border-radius, 5, $multiplier);
    @include px_and_rem(bottom, -1, $multiplier);
    left: 50%;
    @include px_and_rem(margin-left, -1, $multiplier);
  box-sizing: border-box;

    border: #{0.05 * $multiplier} solid rgb(99,99,99);
    border: 0.05rem solid rgb(99,99,99);
    background: #fcfcfc;
}
```

The arrow itself is a more serious business; the basic idea is to use a linear gradient that adds a color only to half the element starting from its diagonal. Then we can rotate the element in order to move the pointed end at its center. The following is the code that needs to be placed within `div[data-arrow]`:

```
&:before{
    position: absolute;
    display: block;
    content: '';
    @include px_and_rem(width, 4, $multiplier);
    @include px_and_rem(height, 0.5, $multiplier);
    @include px_and_rem(bottom, 0.65, $multiplier);
    @include px_and_rem(left, -3, $multiplier);
    background-image: linear-gradient(83.11deg, transparent,
transparent 49%, orange 51%, orange);
    background-image: -webkit-linear-gradient(83.11deg, transparent,
transparent 49%, orange 51%, orange);
    background-image: -moz-linear-gradient(83.11deg, transparent,
transparent 49%, orange 51%, orange);
    background-image: -o-linear-gradient(83.11deg, transparent,
transparent 49%, orange 51%, orange);
```

```
        @include apply-origin(100%, 100%);
        @include transform2d( rotate(-3.45deg));
        box-shadow: 0px #{-0.05 * $multiplier} 0 rgba(0,0,0,0.2);
        box-shadow: 0px -0.05rem 0 rgba(0,0,0,0.2);                    @
    include px_and_rem(border-top-right-radius, 0.25, $multiplier);
        @include px_and_rem(border-bottom-right-radius, 0.35,
    $multiplier);
        }
```

To better understand the trick behind this implementation, we can temporarily add border: 1px solid red within the &:before selector to the result and zoom a bit:

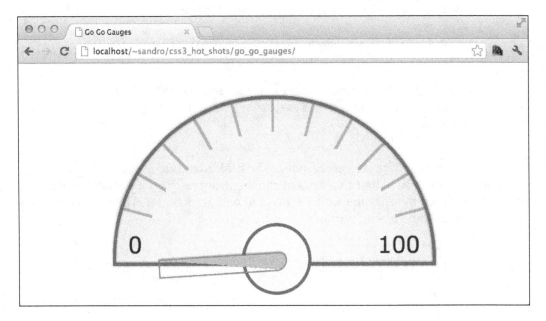

Moving the arrow

Now we want to position the arrow to the correct angle depending on the data-percent attribute value. To do so we have to take advantage of the power of SASS. In theory the CSS3 specification would allow us to valorize some properties using values taken from attributes, but in practice this is only possible while dealing with the content property, as we saw earlier in this book.

So what we're going to do is create a @for loop from 0 to 100 and print in each iteration a selector that matches a defined value of the data-percent attribute. Then we'll set a different rotate() property for each of the CSS rules.

The following is the code; this time it must be placed within the
div[data-gauge] selector:

```
@for $i from 0 through 100 {
    $v: $i;
    @if $i < 10 {
        $v: '0' + $i;
    }

    &[data-percent='#{$v}'] > div[data-arrow] {
        @include transform2d(rotate(#{180deg * $i/100}));
    }
}
```

If you are too scared about the amount of CSS generated, then you can decide to
adjust the increment of the gauge, for example, to 10:

```
@for $i from 0 through 10 {
    &[data-percent='#{$i*10}'] > div[data-arrow] {
        @include transform2d(rotate(#{180deg * $i/10}));
    }
}
```

And the following is the result:

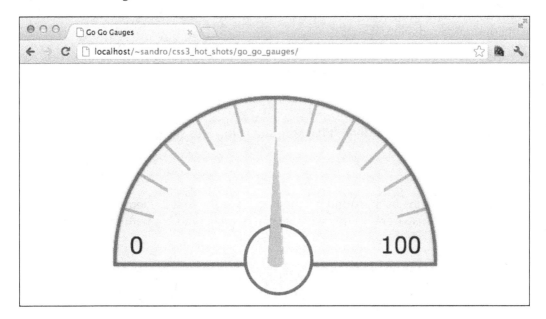

Animating the gauge

We can now animate the arrow using CSS transitions. Basically, we have to tell the browser that the `transform` property needs to be animated; the necessary SASS code is a bit longer than expected because Compass is not yet able to prefix the `transition` property and its value (https://github.com/chriseppstein/compass/issues/289), so we have to do it manually:

```
-webkit-transition: -webkit-transform 0.5s;
-moz-transition: -moz-transform 0.5s;
-ms-transition: -ms-transform 0.5s;
-o-transition: -o-transform 0.5s;
transition: transform 0.5s;
```

After we have placed these CSS instructions inside the `div[data-arrow]` selector, we'll notice that if we change the `data-percentage` property, for example, by using Chrome and its development console, the arrow responds with a smooth animation.

Overall indicator

Some gauges present a color indicator, usually from green to red, associated with the position of the arrow; we can work out a similar result. First of all we need to define two new custom data attributes, one that indicates the percentage at which the indicator switches from green to orange and the other where the percentage switches from orange to red. Here it is:

```
<div data-gauge data-min="0" data-max="100" data-percent="50" data-orange-from="60" data-red-from="90">
  <div data-arrow></div>
</div>
```

Then we need to specify a default background color, let's say `green`, within `div[data-gauge]`:

```
background-color: green;
```

Next, we redefine the background gradient to leave the first 25 percent of the circumference transparent; in this way we can display (and control) the underlying color, so let's rewrite the `gauge-background` call:

```
@include gauge-background(11,
  radial-gradient(50% 100%, circle, rgba(255,255,255,0),
rgba(255,255,255,0) 25%, rgb(255,255,255) 25%, rgb(230,230,230)),
  cover,
  center center
);
```

Now we can use another Sass loop to change the background-color property respecting the value defined in the attributes. Since we're going to implement a loop nested in the previous loop, we have to be careful not to increase the size of the resulting CSS too much.

To achieve this let's consider only the 10s of the data-orange-from and data-red-from data attributes. What we need to do is basically write a CSS rule that activates the red or orange background color if the data-percentage property is greater than or equal to data-orange-from or data-red-from.

The following is the complete loop, including the previous loop we used to move the arrow:

```
@for $i from 0 through 100 {
  $v: $i;
  @if $i < 10 {
    $v: '0' + $i;
  }

  &[data-percent='#{$v}'] > div[data-arrow] {
    @include transform2d(rotate(#{180deg * $i/100}));
  }

  @for $k from 0 through 10 {
    @if $i >= $k * 10 {
      &[data-percent='#{$v}'] [data-orange-from^='#{$k}'] {
        background-color: orange;
      }
      &[data-percent='#{$v}'] [data-red-from^='#{$k}'] {
        background-color: red;
      }
    }
  }
}
```

And following is the result:

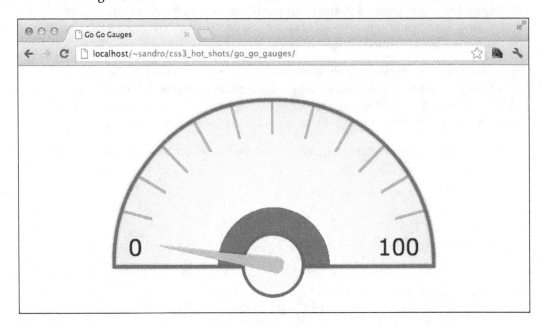

Reducing the size of the CSS

We can reduce the size of the generated CSS by asking Compass to not add a comment before each rule pointing to the corresponding SASS rule. If we want to do that, simply add `line_comments = false` to our `config.rb` file and then stop and relaunch `compass watch` in the project's root folder.

Adding some trembling

As an additional feature we can add an option to let the arrow tremble a bit when it nears 100 percent. We can achieve this behavior by adding a small animation if an extra `data-trembling` attribute is present:

```
<div data-gauge data-min="0" data-max="100" data-percent="50" data-
orange-from="60" data-red-from="90" data-trembling>
```

Unfortunately, Compass doesn't provide CSS3 animation mixins out of the box, so we have to install a Compass plugin that can help us with that. In this case, the plugin is called **compass-animation** (`https://github.com/ericam/compass-animation`), created by Eric Meyer (`http://eric.andmeyer.com/`). This is how it's installed:

```
gem install animation -pre
```

Or as follows:

```
sudo gem install animation --pre
```

And then we have to include the plugin both when calling `compass watch`:

```
compass watch . -r animation
```

And in the header of `application.scss`:

```
@import "animation";
```

Well done! Now we're ready to define a really simple animation that modifies the rotating angle of the arrow causing the trembling effect we're looking for. Let's add a few lines of code at the end of `application.scss`:

```
@include keyframes(trembling) {
    0% {
        @include transform2d( rotate(-5.17deg));
    }
    100% {
        @include transform2d( rotate(-1.725deg));
    }
}
```

Then we need to add a new rule within `div[data-gauge]` that activates this animation if `data-trembling` is present and `data-percentage` starts with 8 or 9 or is equal to `100`:

```
&[data-trembling] [data-percent^='8'] > div[data-arrow]:before,
&[data-trembling] [data-percent^='9'] > div[data-arrow]:before,
&[data-trembling] [data-percent='100'] > div[data-arrow]:before{
    @include animation(trembling 0.2s infinite linear alternate);
}
```

Unfortunately, due to some yet-to-be-resolved bugs in WebKit-based browsers that prevent animations from being applied to before and after pseudo-selectors, at the time of writing only Firefox correctly implements this behavior:

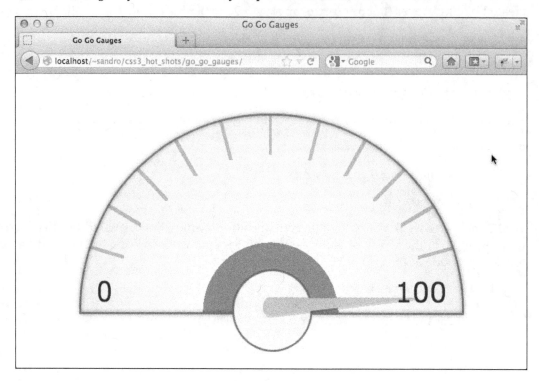

Displaying the gauge value

If we make a small edit to our HTML code, we can easily display the current gauge value:

```
<div data-gauge data-min="0" data-max="100" data-percent="50"
data-orange-from="60" data-red-from="90" data-trembling>
<span>50</span>
  <div data-arrow></div>
</div>
```

And following is the code to add within the div[data-gauge] selector:

```
span{
  display: block;
  color: #DDD;
  @include px_and_rem(font-size, 1.5, $multiplier);
  text-align: center;
```

```
        @include px_and_rem(width, 10, $multiplier);
        @include px_and_rem(height, 5, $multiplier);
        @include px_and_rem(line-height, 5, $multiplier);
    }
```

The result:

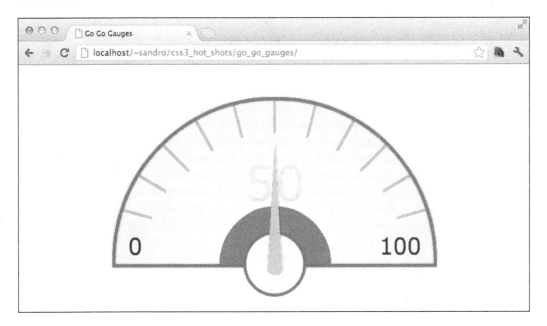

Graceful degradation

To keep this widget meaningful also for those browsers that do not support
background gradients, we have to handle a different representation for the arrow.
To detect where this feature is missing, we can use Modernizr by creating a custom
build (http://modernizr.com/download/), as we saw in the previous chapters that
check only for gradient support:

```
    <script src="js/modernizr.js"></script>
```

Then we can go for a solid background color; the arrow will, of course, become a
rectangle but we'll save the meaning of the widget; let's add this rule at the bottom of
application.scss:

```
    .no-cssgradients div[data-gauge]{

        div[data-arrow]:before{
            background-color: orange;
```

```
        @include transform2d( rotate(0deg));
        box-shadow: none;
        border-radius: 0;
    }
}
```

And following is the result:

We can go a step forward by using Compass' ability to translate gradients into Base64-encoded SVG and use them as fallback background images where native gradients are not supported. Unfortunately, this doesn't work with gradients that express an angle using numeric values, such as 23deg, so we will not be able to reproduce tick marks. We can however ask Compass to convert the radial-gradient property we use for background. The following are the properties we need to add inside the .no-cssgradients div[data-gauge] rule:

```
background-image: -svg(radial-gradient(50% 100%, circle,
rgba(255,255,255,0), rgba(255,255,255,0) 35%, rgb(255,255,255) 35%,
rgb(230,230,230)));
background-size: cover;
background-position: auto;
```

And the following is the result, much closer to the original gauge:

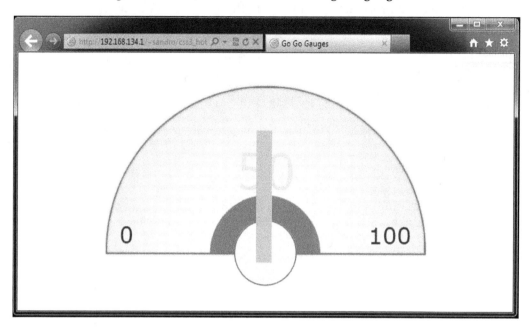

Implementing the gauge in Internet Explorer 8

If we want to support Internet Explorer 8, then we need to address the lack of both the border-radius and transform properties.

For border-radius we can use a JavaScript-based polyfill such as CSS3 Pie, and we can download this polyfill from its website, http://css3pie.com/, and then copy PIE.js in our project's js folder. Next, we can include this JavaScript file from index.html along with the latest version of jQuery and js/application.js, an empty file we are going to use in a while:

```
<!--[if IE 8]>
  <script src="http://code.jquery.com/jquery-1.8.0.min.js"></script>
  <script src="js/PIE.js"></script>
  <script src="js/application.js"></script>
<![endif]-->
```

Usually CSS3 Pie automatically detects how to enhance a given element by identifying the CSS3 properties to emulate. In this case, however, we have used `border-top-left-radius` and `border-top-right-radius` whereas CSS3 Pie only supports the general `border-radius`. We can find a way around this by adding a special `border-radius` property prefixed with `-pie` inside the `div[data-gauge]` rule:

```
-pie-border-radius: #{5 * $multiplier} #{5 * $multiplier} 0px 0px;
```

Next, we have to activate CSS3 Pie by inserting a few lines of JavaScript code inside `js/application.js`:

```
$(function() {
    if (window.PIE) {
        $('div[data-gauge]').each(function() {
            PIE.attach(this);
        });
    }
});
```

And following is the result:

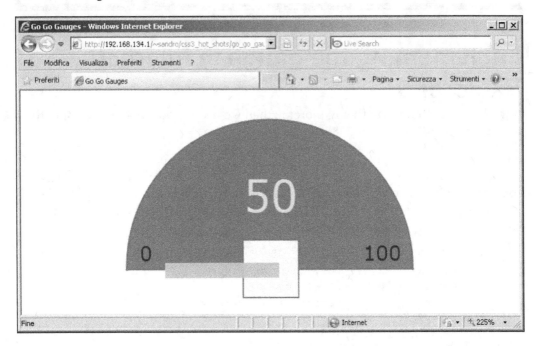

Now if we want to activate the arrow rotation, we need to emulate the `transform` property. To achieve this behavior, we can use `jquery.transform.js` (https:// github.com/louisremi/jquery.transform.js) by Louis-Rémi Babé (http:// twitter.com/louis_remi).

After downloading the library, we need to copy `jquery.transform2d.js` into the `js` folder of our project. Then we add the necessary `script` element in `index.html`. In order to add a different class to the `html` element when the browser is Internet Explorer 8, we will use `IE` conditional comments to add a different class to the `html` element. The following is the result:

```html
<!doctype html>
<!--[if IE 8]> <html class="ie8" > <![endif]-->
<!--[if !IE]> --> <html> <!-- <![endif]-->
<head>
  <title>Go Go Gauges</title>
  <script src="js/modernizr.js"></script>
  <link rel="stylesheet" type="text/css" href="css/application.css">
  <!--[if IE 8]>
    <script src="http://code.jquery.com/jquery-1.8.0.min.js"></script>
    <script src="js/jquery.transform2d.js"></script>
    <script src="js/PIE.js"></script>
    <script src="js/application.js"></script>
  <![endif]-->
</head>
<!-- ...rest of index.html ... -->
```

`jquery.transform2d.js` adds the ability to trigger the `transform` property even on Internet Explorer 8 thereby enhancing the `css` function provided by jQuery; the following is an example:

```js
$(elem).css('transform', 'translate(50px, 30px) rotate(25deg)
scale(2,.5) skewX(-35deg)');
```

So, we can try to add a few more JavaScript lines of code by calling the preceding function; this transforms `js/application.js` as follows:

```js
$(function() {
    if (window.PIE) {
        $('div[data-gauge]').each(function() {
            PIE.attach(this);

            var angle = Math.round(180 * parseInt($(this).attr('data-percent'),10)/100);
            $('div[data-arrow]',$(this)).css({
                'transform': 'rotate(' + angle + 'deg)'
```

```
            });
        });
    }
});
```

Unfortunately, the results are not as good as expected:

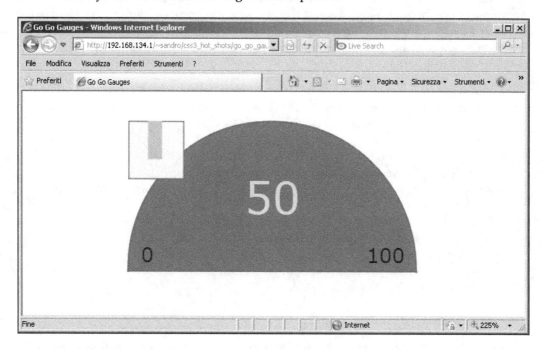

The problem is that the div[data-arrow]:before element is clipped within its parent. This can be resolved by drawing a white disk (now a square) under the arrow, and resizing div[data-arrow] to be as large as the whole widget with a transparent background and no borders in order to easily contain the arrow.

To do so we can use the .ie8 class to add some properties only when the browser is Internet Explorer 8. Let's append a few lines of code to application.scss.

```
.ie8 div[data-gauge]{
  div[data-arrow]{
    width: #{10 * $multiplier};
    height: #{10 * $multiplier};
    margin-top: #{-5 * $multiplier};
    margin-left: #{-5 * $multiplier};
    top: 50%;
    left: 50%;
    background: transparent;
    border: none;
```

```
    &:before{
      bottom: 50%;
      margin-bottom: #{-0.25 * $multiplier};
      left: #{1 * $multiplier};
    }
  }
}
```

And finally, following is the working result:

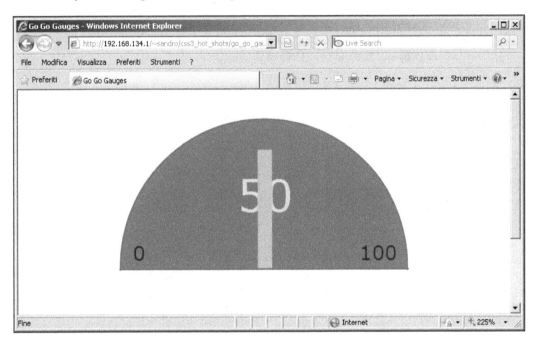

Compass and Internet Explorer 10

The latest version of Compass at the time of writing (0.12.0) doesn't add the -ms-experimental prefix to linear-gradient and radial-gradient. To find a way around this problem and make the gauge work smoothly also on IE10, we have to apply some modifications to our .scss code. In particular, we need to change the gauge-tick-marks function inside _gauge.scss as follows:

```
@function gauge-tick-marks($n, $rest, $ms){
  $linear: null;
  @for $i from 1 through $n {
    $p: -90deg + 180 / ($n+1) * $i;
    $gradient: null;
```

```scss
        @if $ms == true {
          $gradient: -ms-linear-gradient( $p, transparent 46%,
    rgba(99,99,99,0.5) 47%, rgba(99,99,99,0.5) 53%, transparent 54%);
        } @else{
          $gradient: linear-gradient( $p, transparent 46%,
    rgba(99,99,99,0.5) 47%, rgba(99,99,99,0.5) 53%, transparent 54%);
        }
        $linear: append($linear, $gradient, comma);
      }
      @if $ms == true {
        @return append($linear, #{'-ms-' + $rest} );
      } @else{
        @return append($linear, $rest);
      }
    }
```

We also need to change the gauge-background mixin, also inside _gauge.scss:

```scss
@mixin gauge-background($ticks, $rest_gradient, $rest_size, $rest_
position) {

  @include background-image(
    gauge-tick-marks($ticks, $rest_gradient, false)
  );

  background-image: gauge-tick-marks($ticks, $rest_gradient, true);

  background-size: gauge-tick-marks-size($ticks, $rest_size);
  background-position: gauge-tick-marks-position($ticks, $rest_
position);
  background-repeat: no-repeat;
}
```

And finally we have to add an extra CSS line in application.scss inside :before within div[data-arrow]:

```scss
background-image: -ms-linear-gradient(83.11deg, transparent,
transparent 49%, orange 51%, orange);
```

After making these small modifications, we can also appreciate this widget using Internet Explorer 10:

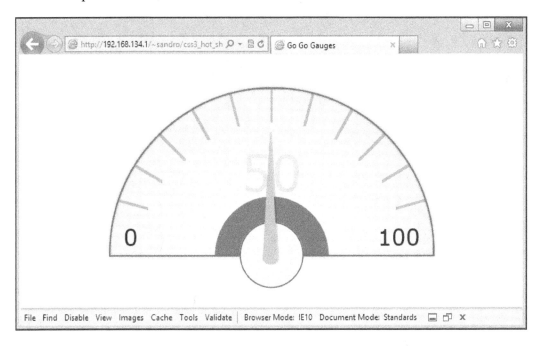

Summary

Drawing a gauge can be more difficult than expected; this is more truer if we also take care of keeping support for older browsers. In this chapter, we learned how to install and work with Compass, create complex CSS using the power of the SASS syntax, and deal with graceful degradation and polyfill techniques. In the next chapter, we'll create a movie trailer by leveraging the power of CSS animations and 3D transforms.

9
Creating an Intro

The goal of this project is to create an intro, a non-interactive animation that uses text and visual effects to present something such as a product, a concept, or whatever. This project gives us the opportunity to explore some advanced animation and 3D topics and to extend our knowledge of Compass while creating some ad hoc functions to handle this complexity.

This chapter will cover the following topics:

- The new flexbox model
- Creating keyframe animations
- Concatenate animations
- Animation of CSS 3D properties

Project description

We want to place some elements in a 3D scene and then move through them. To do so, we first have to create an HTML structure to hold each of these elements, and then we have to find a clever way to obtain the desired effect. But, before doing anything else, we have to define the folder structure and initiate the essential files of the project.

As in the previous project, we'll use SASS and Compass, so we need to install Ruby (http://www.ruby-lang.org/en/downloads/) and then enter `gem install compass` (or `sudo gem install compass`) in the terminal window. After that, we need a `config.rb` file in the root folder of the project containing the Compass configuration:

```
# Require any additional compass plugins here.

# Set this to the root of your project when deployed:
http_path = "YOUR-HTTP-PROJECT-PATH"
```

```
css_dir = "css"
sass_dir = "scss"
images_dir = "img"
javascripts_dir = "js"

# You can select your preferred output style here (can be overridden
via the command line):
# output_style = :expanded or :nested or :compact or :compressed

# To enable relative paths to assets via compass helper functions.
Uncomment:
relative_assets = true

# To disable debugging comments that display the original location of
your selectors. Uncomment:
line_comments = false

preferred_syntax = :sass
```

Well done! The next step is to create the folders required by the project, that is, `css`, `scss`, `img`, and `js` and to define an empty `scss/application.scss` file. We then need to launch `compass watch` . from the project's root folder and finally create the main HTML document, `index.html`.

Creating an HTML structure

What we're going to create is basically a slideshow where each slide is placed in a 3D space and the animation moves from one slide to the other. A basic slide structure can be as simple as:

```
<div data-sequence="1">
  <div data-slide>
    Hello,
  </div>
</div>
```

We need two nested `div` tags to define this structure; the first one will cover 100 percent of the window area, and the second `div` tag will have the necessary properties to hold its content in the center of the screen. Plus, we need to set up each slide so that they will be piled up one above the other because we need them all in the center before we start to move them in the 3D space.

We can use the `flexbox` CSS property to achieve this result. In fact, flexbox has properties to define both vertical and horizontal alignment.

Let's define a basic HTML structure based on what we have seen so far:

```
<!doctype html>
<html>
<head>
  <title>Movie Trailer</title>
  <link href='http://fonts.googleapis.com/css?family=Meie+Script'
rel='stylesheet' type='text/css'>
  <link rel="stylesheet" type="text/css" href="css/application.css">
</head>
<body>
  <div id="viewport">
    <div id="container">

      <div data-sequence="1">
        <div data-slide>
          Hello,
        </div>
      </div>

      <div data-sequence="2">
        <div data-slide>
          this is a demo
        </div>
      </div>

      <div data-sequence="3">
        <div data-slide>
          about the power
        </div>
      </div>

      <div data-sequence="4">
        <div data-slide>
          of CSS 3D
        </div>
      </div>

      <div data-sequence="5">
        <div data-slide>
          and animations
        </div>
      </div>

      <div data-sequence="6">
        <div data-slide>
```

```
            :D
         </div>
       </div>

     </div>
   </div>
 </body>
 </html>
```

Here's what the slides would look like without any CSS:

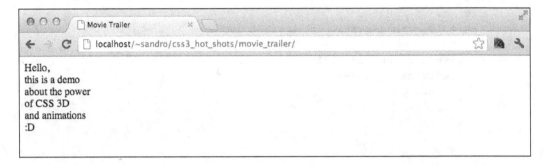

Creating the slide

First of all, let's set each slide's `position` property to `absolute` and `width` and `height` to `100%` by writing a few lines of codes in `scss/application.scss`:

```scss
@import "compass/reset";
@import "compass/css3/box";
@import "compass/css3/transform";


html,body, #viewport, #container{
  height: 100%;
  font-size: 150px;
}

#container{

  & > div{
    width: 100%;
    height: 100%;
    position: absolute;
    top: 0;
    left: 0;
  }
```

```
div[data-slide]{
  width: 100%;
  height: 100%;
  text-align: center;

  @include display-box;
  @include box-align(center);
  @include box-pack(center);
}

}
```

Flexbox is pretty handy, thanks to the `box-pack` and `box-align` properties that basically set the alignment both on the main flexbox direction (horizontal by default, but can be changed with the `box-orient` attribute) and on its perpendicular.

Due to the fact that this project currently works only on Chrome and Firefox (IE10 seems to have some problems using nested 3D transformations), we're ok with these properties; otherwise, we should keep in mind that the old Flexbox syntax (the one from 2009 that we're using) is not supported by Internet Explorer 10.

The latest browser from Microsoft includes support only for the newest Flexbox implementation, which has a rather different syntax and unfortunately doesn't work yet on Gecko-based browsers.

In *Chapter 4, Zooming User Interface*, we developed a project that also worked pretty well in IE10 although we used the unsupported Flexbox syntax. This was because, in that case, we included Flexie, a polyfill that simulates the Flexbox behavior when the old Flexbox syntax is not supported.

Let's dive a bit into the details of this new Flexbox syntax and, for the sake of completeness, let's add both syntaxes to this project.

The new Flexible Box Model

The new flexible layout model (from here onwards, and throughout this chapter, known as Flexbox) is designed, as its previous version, to give the developers a new way of aligning elements on a page.

Elements using this new box model can be laid down vertically or horizontally and can have their order swapped dynamically, plus they can "flex" their sizes and positions to respond to the available spaces.

Here's an example (to test on Internet Explorer 10):

```html
<!DOCTYPE html>

<html lang="en">
    <head>
        <meta charset="utf-8" />
        <title></title>

        <style>
            html,body,ul{
                height: 100%;
                margin: 0;
                padding: 0;
            }
            ul{
                display: -ms-flexbox;
                -ms-flex-direction: row-reverse;
                -ms-flex-pack: center;
                -ms-flex-align: center;
                -ms-flex-wrap: wrap;
            }
            li {
                font-size: 70px;
                line-height: 100px;
                text-align: center;
                list-style-type: none;
                -ms-flex: 1 0 200px;
            }

        </style>

    </head>
    <body>

        <ul>
            <li style="background-color: #f9f0f0">A</li>
            <li style="background-color: #b08b8b">B</li>
            <li style="background-color: #efe195">C</li>
            <li style="background-color: #ccdfc4">D</li>
        </ul>

    </body>
</html>
```

And here's the resulting page:

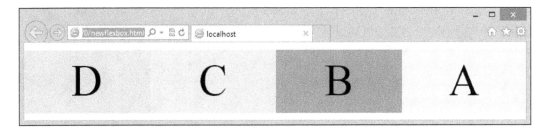

With the previous properties we defined a Flexbox with `display: -ms-flexbox` (the W3C value is `flex`, but every browser alters this value a bit, either by adding a custom prefix or by changing it slightly). We used `-ms-flex-direction: row-reverse` to reverse the visualization order; this property is also used to specify whether we want a horizontal or vertical disposition. The available values are: `row`, `column`, `row-reverse`, and `column-reverse`. The `-ms-flex-pack` and `-ms-flex-align` properties determine the alignment of the Flexbox child elements for both their main and perpendicular axes (as specified with `-ms-flex-direction`).

These properties are still part of the Flexbox IE10 implementation but have recently been replaced by `align-items` and `justify-content`, so we'll also have to take care of this when putting things together.

We used `-ms-flex-wrap: wrap` to ask the browser to dispose the elements on multiple lines if the space on the main axis is not enough to hold them all.

Finally, we used `-ms-flex: 1 0 200px` on each element to indicate that each child has a positive flex factor of `1`, so they will cover empty spaces all at the same speed, keeping their size equal among them, a negative flex factor of `0`, and a preferred size of `200px`.

This, with the `-ms-flex-wrap` property that we specified before, creates an interesting responsive effect, where the elements move to new lines if the browser's window is too small to hold them in a single line:

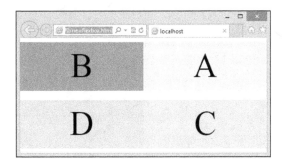

Creating a sample layout

We can benefit from this property to create a three-column layout, where the two lateral columns move under and over the central column if there isn't enough space, such as in a mobile device. Here's the code to create such a layout:

```html
<!DOCTYPE html>

<html lang="en">
    <head>
        <meta charset="utf-8" />
        <title></title>

        <style>
            section {
                min-height: 300px;
            }

            div {
                display: -ms-flexbox;
                -ms-flex-direction: row;
                -ms-flex-pack: center;
                -ms-flex-wrap: wrap;
            }

            aside, nav {
                -ms-flex: 1 3 180px;
                min-height: 100px;
            }

            nav {
                -ms-flex-order: 1;
                 background-color:  #ffa6a6;
            }

            aside {
                -ms-flex-order: 3;
                 background-color:  #81bca1;
            }

            section {
                -ms-flex: 3 1 600px;
                -ms-flex-order: 2;
                background-color: #72c776;
            }
        </style>
    </head>
    <body>
```

```
    <div>
        <section></section>
        <nav></nav>
        <aside></aside>
    </div>

    </body>
</html>
```

And here's the result:

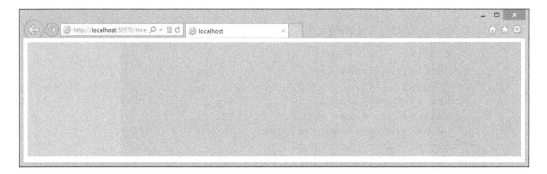

If we now resize the browser window, we'll notice how the `nav` and `aside` element moves over and under the main content, creating a nice layout for mobile devices:

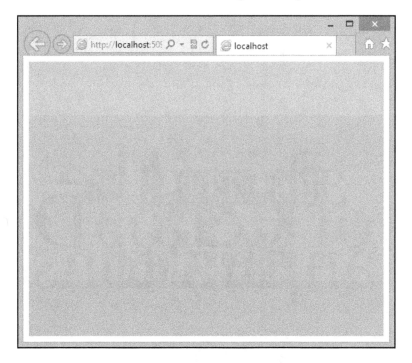

Let's step back to our project; we can easily add support for this new version of Flexbox with a few lines of CSS, as follows:

```
div[data-slide]{
  width: 100%;
  height: 100%;
  text-align: center;

  @include display-box;
  @include box-align(center);
  @include box-pack(center);

    display: -ms-flexbox;
    display: -moz-flex;
    display: -webkit-flex;
    display: flex;
    -ms-flex-pack: center;
    -moz-align-items: center;
    -webkit-align-items: center;
    align-items: center;
    -ms-flex-align: center;
    -moz-justify-content: center;
    -webkit-justify-content: center;
    justify-content: center;
}
```

And here's the much-awaited result:

Disposing the slides

We can now use some 3D `transform` properties to move and rotate each of these slides in a 3D scene. These transformations are absolutely arbitrary and can be chosen to suit the movie trailer's overall effect; here's an example:

```
div{
  &[data-sequence="1"]{
    @include transform(rotateX(45deg));
  }

  &[data-sequence="2"]{
    @include transform(rotateY(45deg) translateY(300px) scale(0.5));
  }

  &[data-sequence="3"]{
    @include transform(rotateX(90deg) translateY(300px) scale(0.5));
  }

  &[data-sequence="4"]{
    @include transform(rotateX(90deg) translateY(300px)
translateX(600px) scale(0.5));
  }

  &[data-sequence="5"]{
    @include transform(rotateX(90deg) translateZ(300px)
translateY(350px) translateX(600px) scale(0.5));
  }

  &[data-sequence="6"]{
    @include transform(rotateZ(30deg) translateY(500px)
translateZ(300px));
  }
}
```

Now, we need to set some 3D standard properties such as `transform-style` and `perspective` on the slide's parent elements:

```
#viewport{
  @include transform-style(preserve-3d);
  @include perspective(500px);
  overflow: hidden;
  width: 100%;
}

#container{
    @include transform-style(preserve-3d);
}
```

If we now run the project in Chrome, we will notice that the slides are not piled up like in the Previous screenshot; rather, they are now placed all around the 3D scene (most of them are not visible after the transformations):

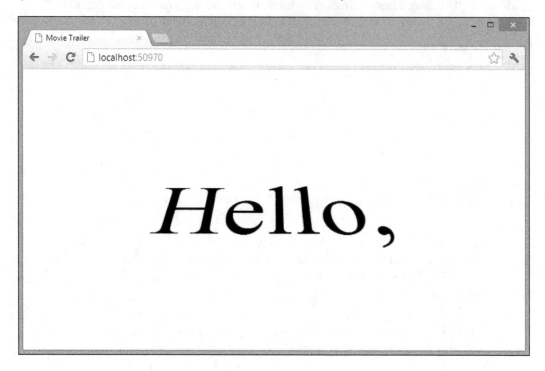

Moving the camera

Now, we'll learn to create the effect of a camera that moves through the slides; due to the fact that we cannot move the user's viewport, we'll need to simulate this feeling by moving the elements on the scene; this can be achieved by applying some transformations to #container.

To move the camera close to a slide, we need to apply the exact transformations we used on that slide, but with opposite values and in the reverse order. So, for example, if we want to view the frame whose data-sequence property is 3, we can write:

```
// not to be permanently added to the project
#container{
    @include transform(scale(2) translateY(-300px) rotateX(-90deg));
}
```

Here's the result:

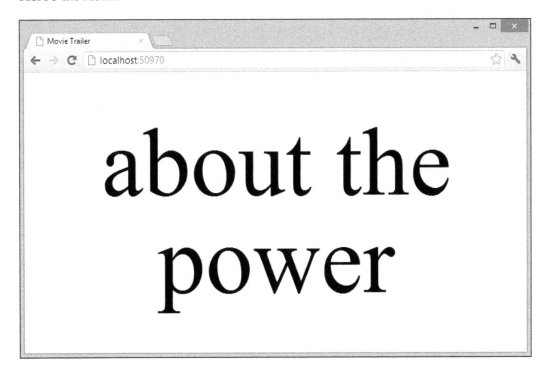

The animation has to focus on a slide, stay still for some time, and then move to the next slide. When creating this kind of effect, we usually face the following two main problems:

- CSS `keyframes` accepts only percentage values, but we'd rather prefer to use seconds as a measurement unit (for example, to say "move to the next slide in 2 seconds and then stay still for 1 second")
- We need to handle two `keyframes` rules for each slide (moving and still); it would be better to have a function that handles this for us

We can easily solve both these problems by using SASS. First, we can create a function that converts seconds to a percentage value by accepting the total length of the animation:

```
$total_animation_duration: 11.5;
@function sec_to_per($sec, $dur: $total_animation_duration){
  @return 0% + $sec * 100 / $dur;
}
```

This function takes two arguments—the value we want to convert from seconds to percentage and the total length of the animation. If this argument is not provided, the value is then set equal to the `$total_animation_duration` variable.

The second function that we can create for this project takes the `move` time and `still` time as arguments and prints the necessary keyframes as well as keeping track of the percentage of advancement of the animation:

```
$current_percentage: 0%;
@mixin animate_to_and_wait($move, $still ) {

    $move_increment: sec_to_per($move);
    $current_percentage: $current_percentage + $move_increment;

    #{ $current_percentage }{ @content }

    @if $still == end {
      $current_percentage: 100%;
    } @else{
      $still_increment: sec_to_per($still);
      $current_percentage: $current_percentage + $still_increment;
    }

    #{ $current_percentage }{ @content }

}
```

What this function does is to basically transform the `$move` parameter in percentage and add this value to the `$current_percentage` global variable that keeps track of the advancements in the animation.

We then print a keyframe, using the percentage that we just computed, containing the value of the `@content` variable that SASS fills for us with the contents we put between the curly brackets after a function call, for example:

```
myfunction(arg1, arg2){
    // everything here is placed into @content variable
}
```

If `$still` is equal to `end`, we want the still phase to last until the end of the animation, so we set the `$current_percentage` variable to `100%`; otherwise, we treat this variable the same as we treated the `$move` variable and then print another keyframe.

Fun with animations

To handle all the experimental prefixes that come with CSS3 animation properties, we can again use the Compass animation plugin (`gem install animation` from the command-line terminal, and then relaunch Compass using `compass watch . -r animation` from the project's root folder).

We also need to include `animation` in `application.scss`:

```
@import "animation";
```

And we also need to write a small function that wraps the function provided by the animation plugin and reset `$current_percentage` each time it switches from one experimental prefix to the other:

```
@mixin ext_keyframes($name){

  @include with-only-support-for($moz: true) {
    @-moz-keyframes #{$name} { @content; }
  }
  $current_percentage: 0%;
  @include with-only-support-for($webkit: true) {
      @-webkit-keyframes #{$name} { @content; }
  }
  $current_percentage: 0%;
  @include with-only-support-for {
    @keyframes #{$name} { @content; }
  }
}
```

Good! We're now ready to put things together and define our animation:

```
/* == [BEGIN] Camera == */
@include ext_keyframes(camera){
  0%{
    @include transform(none);
  }

  @include animate_to_and_wait(0.5, 1.5){
    @include transform(scale(2) rotateX(-45deg));
  }

  @include animate_to_and_wait(0.5, 1.5){
    @include transform(scale(2) translateY(-300px) rotateY(-45deg));
  }

  @include animate_to_and_wait(0.5, 1.5){
    @include transform(scale(2) translateY(-300px) rotateX(-90deg));
  }
```

```
    @include animate_to_and_wait(0.5, 1.5){
        @include transform(scale(2) translateX(-600px) translateY(-300px)
    rotateX(-90deg));
    }

    @include animate_to_and_wait(0.5, 1.5){
        @include transform(scale(2) translateX(-600px) translateY(-350px)
    translateZ(-300px) rotateX(-90deg));
    }

    @include animate_to_and_wait(0.5, end){
        @include transform(scale(2) translateZ(-300px) translateY(-500px)
    rotateZ(-30deg));
    }
}
/* == [END] Camera == */
```

Lastly, we have to add the appropriate animation property to `#container`:

```
#container{
@include animation(camera #{0s + $total_animation_duration} linear);
@include animation-fill-mode(forwards);
}
```

Done! A last reload in the browser is enough to fully appreciate the animation:

Step animations

We'll now create a special animation that switches the background color of our project synchronously with each slide change. Since we don't want any fading between colors, we'll introduce step animation.

Step animations let us specify how many frames must be placed between each declared keyframe; here's an example:

```
<!DOCTYPE html>

<html lang="en">
    <head>
        <meta charset="utf-8" />
        <title></title>
        <style>
            div {
                width:  100px;
                height: 100px;
                background-color: red;
                position: absolute;
                -webkit-animation: diagonal 3s steps(5) infinite
alternate;
            }

            @-webkit-keyframes diagonal {
                from {
                    top: 0;
                    left: 0;
                }
                to {
                    top: 500px;
                    left: 500px;
                }
            }

        </style>
    </head>
    <body>
        <div></div>
    </body>
</html>
```

If we now run this small example in a browser, we'll see that the movement of the div element is not fluid, but composed of only five frames. We can add a special keyword start or end to the step declaration (for example, step(5, end)) to ask the browser to skip the initial or the final keyframe during each step. Good! Now, we can apply the same concept to our intro project. First of all, we need to define an animation that changes the background-color property:

```scss
/* == [BEGIN] bg == */
@include ext_keyframes(bg){
  0%{
    background: green;
  }
  #{sec_to_per(2)}{
    background: darkolivegreen;
  }
  #{sec_to_per(4)}{
    background: violet;
  }
  #{sec_to_per(6)}{
    background: orange;
  }
  #{sec_to_per(8)}{
    background: lightsteelblue;
  }
  #{sec_to_per(10)}{
    background: thistle;
  }
  100%{
    background: pink;
  }
}
/* == [END] bg == */
```

Please note how we used the sec_to_per function in order to use seconds instead of percentages; next, we just need to add bg to #viewport using the animation property:

```scss
#viewport{
  @include animation(bg #{0s + $total_animation_duration}
steps(1,start));
  @include animation-fill-mode(forwards);
}
```

And here's the result:

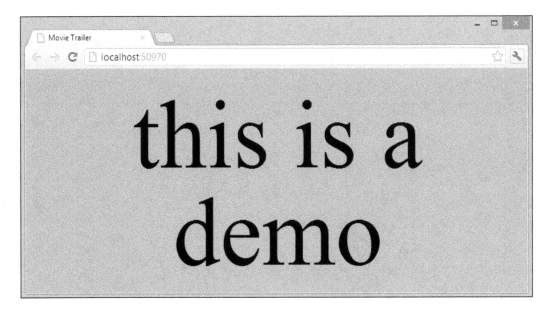

Final touches

Now that we have a basic structure defined and have learned how to create a fluid animation that moves through the slides placed in a 3D scene, the next step, obviously, is to enrich each of these slides with images, videos, graphs, and everything we might need to fulfill our purposes.

To do so, we can use the knowledge already accumulated during the previous chapters of this book; for example, we can easily define a fade-in animation for the first slide, as follows:

```
div[data-sequence="1"]{
  @include animation(sequence_1 2s linear);
  @include animation-fill-mode(forwards);
}

/* == [BEGIN] sequence_1 == */
@include ext_keyframes(sequence_1){
  0%{
    color: rgba(0,0,0,0);
  }
}
/* == [END] sequence_1 == */
```

We can also add custom fonts to our slides:

```
div[data-sequence="2"]{
    font-family: 'Meie Script', cursive;
}
```

Here's the result:

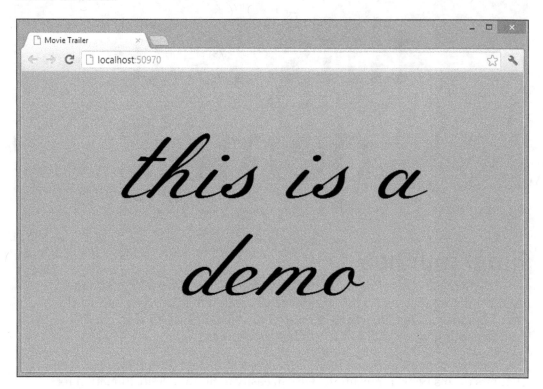

Summary

CSS animations and 3D transformations can be combined to create interesting results; of course, when we move to these types of features, we have to accept the fact that some browsers may not be able to support the project. However, we can always use some feature detection library, such as Modernizr, to address this issue by providing some alternative visualization when these features are not supported.

In the next chapter, we'll create a nice graph library entirely with CSS3!

10
CSS Charting

With just a simple Google search, we discover that there are plenty of amazing charting libraries around, such as **Google Chart Tools** (`https://developers.google.com/chart/`), **Highcharts** (`http://www.highcharts.com/`), and **gRaphael** (`http://g.raphaeljs.com/`), to name a few. What we might not know is that there are some CSS techniques that allow us to create fully functional charts without using JavaScript libraries. In this chapter, we'll explore some of these techniques, here are the topics:

- Creating a bar chart
- Implementing a cross-browser, flexible box layout
- Handling and displaying `data-*` attributes
- Implementing advanced gradients
- Adding more chart series
- Animating the chart
- Creating a pie chart

Creating a bar chart

To create a bar chart, we need to set up an array of `div` elements all aligned to their bottom and then control their height properties. Then, we need to find a clever way to display each bar's label and, optionally, each bar's value.

To create the `div` array, we could simply use a `div` container with `position:relative` containing a `div` element for each bar absolutely positioned with `bottom:0`. The problem with this technique is that we have to define the size of each bar in the CSS. We would also need to know in advance the number of bars of the chart we're styling, making our CSS less adaptable with different charts or dynamic modification of the chart that we're styling.

To solve this problem, we need to find a CSS structure that can equally subdivide the container's space between the children elements. We've already used the flexible box layout display mode in past chapters, however, we've typically used it for centering elements both horizontally and vertically. To solve our bar graph positioning issue is when the flexible box layout proves to be invaluable.

Let's define an `index.html` file with a structure to develop our project, as follows:

```html
<!doctype html>
<html>
<head>
<meta charset="utf-8">
  <title>Charts</title>
  <link rel="stylesheet" type="text/css" href="css/application.css">
</head>
<body>
    <div data-bar-chart class="this_bar_chart">
        <div data-bar data-label="mon">
            <div class="value series1" data-value-percentage="40"
data-value-label="40"></div>
        </div>
        <div data-bar data-label="tue">
            <div class="value series1" data-value-percentage="100"
data-value-label="125"></div>
        </div>
        <div data-bar data-label="wed">
            <div class="value series1" data-value-percentage="80"
data-value-label="112"></div>
        </div>
        <div data-bar data-label="thu">
            <div class="value series1" data-value-percentage="15"
data-value-label="21"></div>
        </div>
        <div data-bar data-label="fri">
            <div class="value series1" data-value-percentage="10"
data-value-label="14"></div>
        </div>
        <div data-bar data-label="sat">
            <div class="value series1" data-value-percentage="35"
data-value-label="46"></div>
        </div>
        <div data-bar data-label="sun">
            <div class="value series1" data-value-percentage="58"
data-value-label="67"></div>
        </div>
    </div>
</body>
```

Here, we can recognize three distinct components of this structure. First of all the `div` element with a `data-bar-chart` attribute; this is the container of the whole chart; it also holds all the bars. Then, we have the `div` elements with the `data-bar` attribute; each of them keeps the necessary space for the real bar chart within the container and hold the corresponding bar label in the `data-label` attribute.

Lastly, the `div` elements with the `.value` class represent the actual bar of the chart; the height of the bar is expressed with the `data-value-percentage` attribute, which ranges from `0%` to `100%`. We decided to go for a normalized value because this keeps our chart CSS implementation more generic and not fixed on this particular instance. To express the real value of each bar, we have defined another attribute, `data-value-label`.

Before we begin, we need to set up, as usual, our development environment, so we need to create some folders in the root folder of our project, namely, `css`, `img`, `js`, and `scss`. We'll use Sass and Compass for this project, so we need to install them (if this has not already been done) by first installing Ruby (`http://www.ruby-lang.org/en/downloads/`) and then executing `gem install compass` (or `sudo gem install compass`) from the command-line terminal.

Lastly, we need to create a `config.rb` file in the root folder of the project, which can be done by copying the same file from the previous project.

When everything has been set up, we can create an `application.scss` file under the `scss` folder containing only the following line:

```
@import "compass/reset";
```

We then can enter `compass watch .` from the command-line terminal and verify the presence of a corresponding `css/application.css` file.

Subdividing the space

Because we don't want to develop a CSS bar chart implementation that only works for this specific HTML code, we have to distinguish between properties related to this chart from ones that are more generic and re-usable. For this reason, the main element has a class called `this_bar_chart`. We can use this class specifically for this chart, for example, to define `width` and `height` for this chart, thus we can write the following in `application.scss`:

```
.this_bar_chart{
    width: 600px;
    height: 400px;
}
```

Good! We now need to implement the flexible box layout to subdivide the spaces of elements with the data-bar-chart attribute equally between all the data-bar elements.

A minor complication is that there are currently two distinct flexbox syntaxes (as we saw in *Chapter 9, Creating an Intro*), and browser support for both syntaxes is incomplete. To work around this complication, we will implement both. We need to set the container's display property to either box (old syntax) or flex (new syntax) and then set a property box-flex: 1 (old syntax) or flex: 1 (new syntax) for each data-bar element.

By specifying that each data-bar element has the same flex grow factor, all of these elements will synchronize to fill the container space at the same speed, resulting in the same width for each element.

Here is the code to add to application.scss:

```scss
*[data-bar-chart]{
    display: -moz-box;
    display: -webkit-box;
    display: box;

    display: -moz-flex;
    display: -webkit-flex;
    display: -ms-flexbox;
    display: flex;

    /* temporary property only for this step */
    border: 1px solid black;

    *[data-bar]{
        -webkit-box-flex: 1;
        -moz-box-flex: 1;
        box-flex: 1;

        -moz-flex: 1;
        -webkit-flex: 1;
        -ms-flex: 1;
        flex: 1;

        /* temporary property only for this step */
        border: 1px solid black;
    }
}
```

If we try our project in a browser (Chrome, Firefox, Internet Explorer 10), we'll notice how the container space gets equally subdivided between all the children, whatever the number:

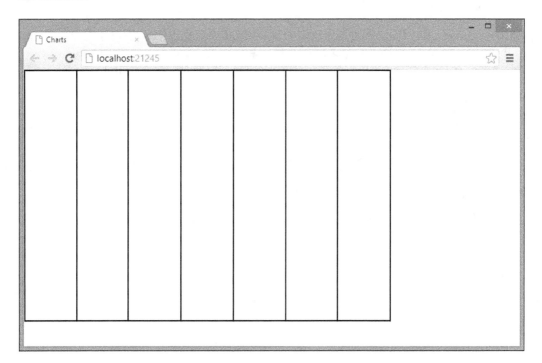

Adding Internet Explorer 8 and 9 support

Internet Explorer versions prior to Version 10 do not support flexbox in any of its forms. We can easily find a way around this problem by using a polyfill library (which we have already introduced in *Chapter 4, Zooming User Interface*) named flexie.js (http://flexiejs.com/).

To add flexie, we need to first download jQuery (http://jquery.com/), then Selectivzr (http://selectivizr.com/), and finally flexie itself. All of these three files must be placed within the js folder.

Finally, we can place these three files within a conditional comment, ensuring that only Internet Explorer 8 and 9 need to perform these additional HTTP requests:

```
<!--[if (gte IE 8)&(lte IE 9)]>
    <script src="js/jquery-1.8.2.min.js"></script>
    <script src="js/selectivizr-min.js"></script>
    <script src="js/flexie.js"></script>
<![endif]-->
```

Creating bar labels

Good! We can now remove the temporary border properties and move on to the next step, creating bar labels.

At the moment, our bar labels are contained within the data-bar element as values of the data-label attribute, so we have to use an :after or :before pseudo selector in conjunction with a content property to be able to print them.

We also need to reserve some space for those labels, because, at the moment, all of the container's height is occupied by the bars of the chart to be created.

We can achieve this by adding padding-bottom to the container (along with a box-sizing property to keep the original container height, where supported) and then placing the bar label outside and below each data-bar element, using absolute positioning.

Here's the small chunk of CSS code we can implement to achieve this behavior:

```
@import "compass/css3/box-sizing";

*[data-bar-chart]{
    padding-bottom: 30px;
    @include box-sizing(border-box);

    /* temporary property only for this step */
    border: 1px solid red;

    *[data-bar]{
        position: relative;

        /* temporary property only for this step */
        background: green;

        &:before{
            display: block;
            content: attr(data-label);
            position: absolute;
            top: 100%;
            left: 0;
            width: 100%;
            text-align: center;
            padding-top: 10px;
        }
    }
}
```

We used the `top:100%` property to move the `:before` selector's content outside the containing element without specifying a precise height value, by doing this, we keep our CSS chart instructions as generic as possible.

Reloading the project in the browser now shows the labels correctly placed at the bottom of the container, within its padding space:

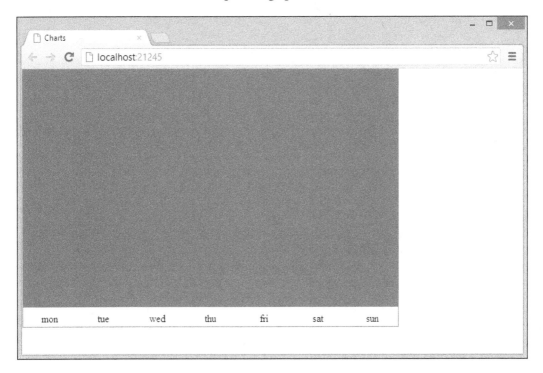

Before moving on, we need to remember to remove the temporary properties that we defined during this step.

Designing the bars

Each bar contains a `.value` element, this element needs to be styled to respond to the following characteristics:

- Its height must conform to its `data-value-percentage` value
- It must be aligned on the bottom of its parent `data-bar` element
- It must show somewhere the value of its `data-value-label` value
- It must have some sort of margin between itself and the next chart bar

Let's start with these last two points. First, we can use absolute positioning to place the .value element at the bottom of its parent and at a chosen distance from its parent's right and left borders.

Here's the required CSS:

```
.value{
    position: absolute;
    bottom: 0;
    left: 6%;
    right: 6%;
}
```

The required behavior regarding the height of the bar can be achieved by looping from 0 to 100 and printing a CSS rule that sets the height property according to the current loop index as follows:

```
@for $i from 0 through 100{
    *[data-value-percentage='#{$i}']{ height: 0% + $i; }
}
```

Finally, we can use the same trick that we implemented with the chart labels to print each bar value, only this time, we need to place the text just over each colored bar. We also have to remember that, as with labels, we need to save some space for this text in case the bar's height property is set to 100%; therefore, we need to add a top padding (using the padding-top property) to the container, as follows:

```
*[data-bar-chart]{
    padding-top: 35px;

    .value:after{
        content: attr(data-value-label);
        position: absolute;
        font-size: 25px;
        display: block;
        bottom: 100%;
        padding-bottom: 10px;
        left: 0;
        width: 100%;
        text-align: center;
    }
}
```

Before showcasing the project, we need to provide at least one color for the chart bars, this is another temporary property because we're going to replace it when we introduce chart series later in this chapter.

```
.value{
    /* temporary property only for this step */
    background: green;
}
```

After a reload in our favorite browser, our project looks like this:

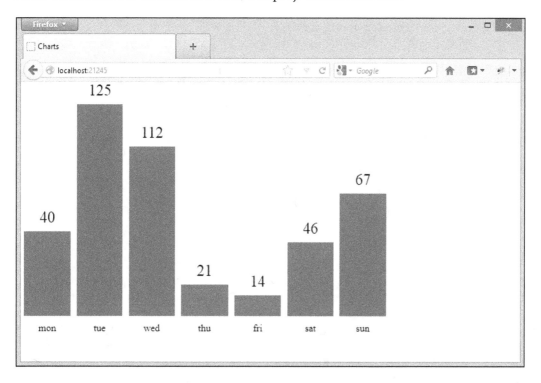

Beautifying the chart

Now it's time to remove the temporary properties and beautify the chart a bit.

There are many ways by which we can further beautify what we've done so far and make it look even better. First of all, we can use a custom font for both labels and bar values; next, we can add rounded corners and shadows. Finally, we can use gradients.

On the subject of gradients, we can implement a technique similar to the one we used in *Chapter 2, Shiny Buttons*, where we used gradients to handle highlights and shadows, setting the `background-color` property to the color of the bar.

Moving forward, we will choose a custom font, set some inset shadows, specify a `border-radius` property, and then define a gradient that goes from transparent to a solid color; here's the required CSS:

```
@import url(http://fonts.googleapis.com/css?family=Chivo);
@import "compass/css3/images";

.value:after, *[data-bar]:before{
    font-family: 'Chivo', sans-serif;
}

.value{
    background-image: -ms-linear-gradient(bottom, transparent,
rgba(0,0,0,0.3));
    @include background-image(linear-gradient(bottom, transparent,
rgba(0,0,0,0.3)));
    border-top-left-radius: 5px;
    border-top-right-radius: 5px;
    box-shadow: 1px 1px 0px rgb(255,255,255) inset;
    border: 1px solid rgba(0,0,0,0.5);
    @include box-sizing(border-box);
}
```

We have to specify `-ms-linear-gradient` explicitly because Compass doesn't handle the `-ms-` experimental prefix for this kind of property. This behavior by Compass is in fact correct, because Microsoft stated that most of the latest CSS3 properties work unprefixed on the new Internet Explorer (`http://blogs.msdn.com/b/ie/archive/2012/06/06/moving-the-stable-web-forward-in-ie10-release-preview.aspx`), but at the time of writing, the current version of Internet Explorer 10 still requires the `-ms-` prefix.

Now, we can test out the project by simply adding a temporary `background-color` property to the `.value` element, as follows:

```
.value{
    /* temporary property only for this step */
    background-color: green;
}
```

And here's the result:

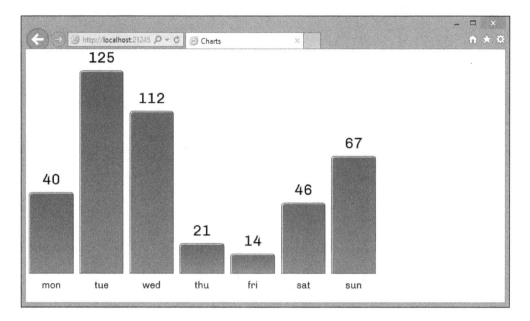

Results may vary on browsers that don't support the properties we've used to beautify the project. However, since the `background-color` property is set to the main color, key information from the chart is still available.

Chart lines

We can also use background properties to draw the horizontal lines that usually mark and divide the background of a bar chart into steps, each representing 20 percent of the total height.

To proceed, we need to create a linear gradient that is mostly transparent, except for its very first pixel, and then we have to set the size of this background to 20 percent and repeat it; here's the required CSS:

```
*[data-bar]{
    background-image: -ms-linear-gradient(top, rgb(99,99,99),
rgb(99,99,99) 1px, transparent 1px, transparent);
    @include background-image(linear-gradient(top, rgb(99,99,99),
rgb(99,99,99) 1px, transparent 1px, transparent));
    background-size: 100% 25%;
    background-repeat: repeat-y;
}
```

And here's the result:

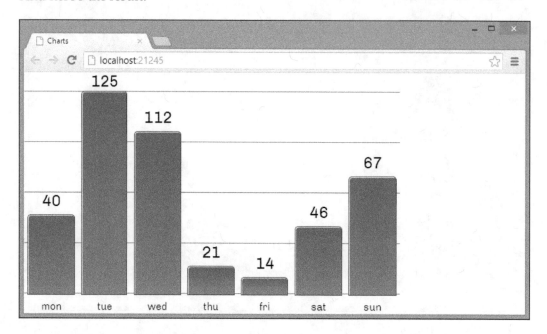

This is not exactly what we were expecting; the last line is slightly higher up than the bottom of the bar. This is probably because the browser finds it difficult to align a repeating gradient when the container size is not a perfect multiplier of the number of times we want the background to fit.

We can try a different approach using a single gradient describing five small gray bands; here's the CSS code that replaces the previous one:

```
*[data-bar]{
    background-image: -ms-linear-gradient(top, rgb(150,150,150),
rgb(150,150,150) 0.5%, transparent 0.5%, transparent 24.5%,
rgb(150,150,150) 24.5%, rgb(150,150,150) 25%, transparent 25%,
transparent 49.5%, rgb(150,150,150) 49.5%, rgb(150,150,150)
50%, transparent 50%, transparent 74.5%, rgb(150,150,150) 74.5%,
rgb(150,150,150) 75%, transparent 75%, transparent 99.5%,
rgb(150,150,150) 99.5%, rgb(150,150,150) 100%);
    @include background-image(linear-gradient(top, rgb(150,150,150),
rgb(150,150,150) 0.5%, transparent 0.5%, transparent 24.5%,
rgb(150,150,150) 24.5%, rgb(150,150,150) 25%, transparent 25%,
transparent 49.5%, rgb(150,150,150) 49.5%, rgb(150,150,150)
50%, transparent 50%, transparent 74.5%, rgb(150,150,150) 74.5%,
rgb(150,150,150) 75%, transparent 75%, transparent 99.5%,
rgb(150,150,150) 99.5%, rgb(150,150,150) 100%));
}
```

Although the code appears less elegant, the results are far better than the previous attempt.

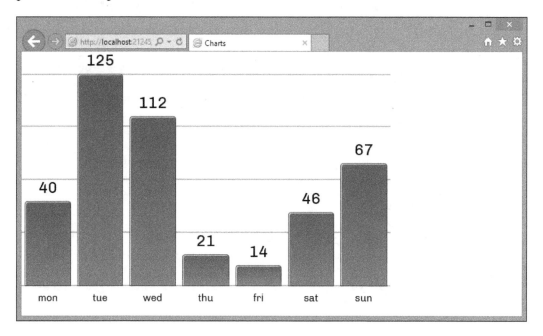

Our current solution is not entirely perfect because we are forced to specify the size of the gray bands using percentages, and this may lead to thick bands when the size of the chart increases too much. All things considered, this is the best solution so far, so let's stick with it.

Now we can remove the temporary CSS `background-color` property and move to the next chart enhancement, the series.

Chart series

In our markup, all the `.value` elements have another class, `.series1`; this is because we want our chart to support multiple series, so let's add to our markup a new `.series2` set of elements:

```
<input type="checkbox" class="series1" checked id="series1"> <label
for="series1">show serie 1</label>
<input type="checkbox" class="series2" checked id="series2"> <label
for="series2">show serie 2</label><br/>
<div data-bar-chart class="this_bar_chart">
    <div data-bar data-label="mon">
```

```
            <div class="value series1" data-value-percentage="40" data-
value-label="40"></div>
            <div class="value series2" data-value-percentage="60" data-
value-label="60"></div>
        </div>
        <div data-bar data-label="tue">
            <div class="value series1" data-value-percentage="100" data-
value-label="125"></div>
            <div class="value series2" data-value-percentage="30" data-
value-label="20"></div>
        </div>
        <div data-bar data-label="wed">
            <div class="value series1" data-value-percentage="80" data-
value-label="112"></div>
            <div class="value series2" data-value-percentage="70" data-
value-label="80"></div>
        </div>
        <div data-bar data-label="thu">
            <div class="value series1" data-value-percentage="15" data-
value-label="21"></div>
            <div class="value series2" data-value-percentage="50" data-
value-label="60"></div>
        </div>
        <div data-bar data-label="fri">
            <div class="value series1" data-value-percentage="10" data-
value-label="14"></div>
            <div class="value series2" data-value-percentage="90" data-
value-label="100"></div>
        </div>
        <div data-bar data-label="sat">
            <div class="value series1" data-value-percentage="35" data-
value-label="46"></div>
            <div class="value series2" data-value-percentage="20" data-
value-label="25"></div>
        </div>
        <div data-bar data-label="sun">
            <div class="value series1" data-value-percentage="58" data-
value-label="67"></div>
            <div class="value series2" data-value-percentage="10" data-
value-label="12"></div>
        </div>
    </div>
```

We can assume that each chart series comes with a checkbox and a bunch of elements, all with the same `.seriesx` class, where x is a number between 1 and 4 (we don't support more than 4 series for each chart).

With this assumption, we can set up a Sass `@for` loop between 1 and 4 to accomplish the following tasks:

- Set `background-color` for the series
- Hide the series if the corresponding checkbox is not checked

To dynamically create different colors for each series, we can rely on the **hsl** coordinate system (**hue saturation lightness**) because by simply changing the hue component, we can obtain colors that keep the same saturation and lightness, resulting in a more pleasant composition.

To hide the series, we have to create a rather complex CSS rule that basically says that, if the checkbox with a class—say `series1`—is checked, get all the elements within the `data-bar-chart` series with the same series class (`series1` in this case) and set their `opacity` properties to 1.

Here's the corresponding CSS:

```
.value{
    opacity: 0;
}

@for $i from 1 through 4{
    input:checked.series#{$i}[type='checkbox'] ~ *[data-bar-chart]
.series#{$i}{
        opacity: 1;
    }
    *[data-bar-chart] .series#{$i}{
        background-color: hsl(0deg + 10 * $i, 50%, 50%);
    }
}
```

And here's the result:

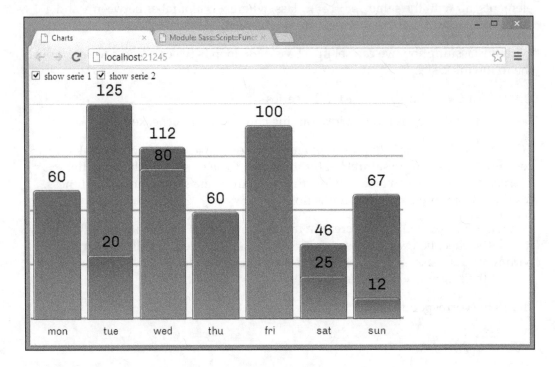

Adding some animations

We have used `opacity` to hide the series in response to the checkbox uncheck so that we can add a `transition` directive and fade in and out the series:

```
@import "compass/css3/transition";

.value{
    @include transition(opacity 0.4s);
}
```

Internet Explorer 8 and 9

Surprisingly, even Internet Explorer 8 understands and applies the complex rule that we defined before. The credit for this achievement goes to Selectivzr, a library we included with flexie and that has the ability to enable some CSS3 selectors from IE6 to IE8. The only problem is that these browsers don't support the `opacity` property, so we have to detect this and switch back to the better supported `display:none` property.

We can use a custom Modernizr build to accomplish this task, so let's download it from the official website (http://modernizr.com/download) taking care to select the **opacity** checkbox from the **CSS3** column.

Next, after having renamed the file to just modernizr.js, we can include it in the HTML file, as follows:

```
<script src="js/modernizr.js"></script>
```

Finally, we need to add another rule within the series' loop that uses display:none instead of opacity: 0 if the class no-opacity is present on the html element.

Here's the new loop, including the .no-opacity selector:

```
.value{
    opacity: 0;
}

@for $i from 1 through 4{
    input[type='checkbox'].series#{$i}:not(:checked) ~ *[data-bar-
chart] .series#{$i}{
        opacity: 1;
    }

    .no-opacity input[type='checkbox'].series#{$i}:not(:checked) ~
*[data-bar-chart] .series#{$i}{
        display:none;
    }

    *[data-bar-chart] .series#{$i}{
        background-color: hsl(0deg + 10 * $i, 50%, 50%);
    }
}
```

Rotating the chart

By taking advantage of the CSS transform property, we can easily transform this chart from a vertical bar chart to a horizontal one. This process, however, cannot be defined generically, as we did for bars and series, because it is closely dependent upon the chart size; so, we'll use the .this_bar_chart selector.

To accomplish this, we'll change the width and height properties of the chart (we'll set them both to 500px to better handle the sub-sequential rotation), rotate the whole chart by 90 degrees, and then rotate back the text elements in order to keep them readable.

Here's the CSS:

```
@import "compass/css3/transform";

.this_bar_chart{
    @include transform(rotate(90deg) translate(10px,-10px));
    width: 500px;
    height: 500px;

    *[data-bar]{

        &:before{
            @include transform(rotate(-90deg) translate(-7px,0px));
        }

        .value:after{
            @include transform(rotate(-90deg) translate( 5px ,0px));
        }
    }
}
```

And this is the result:

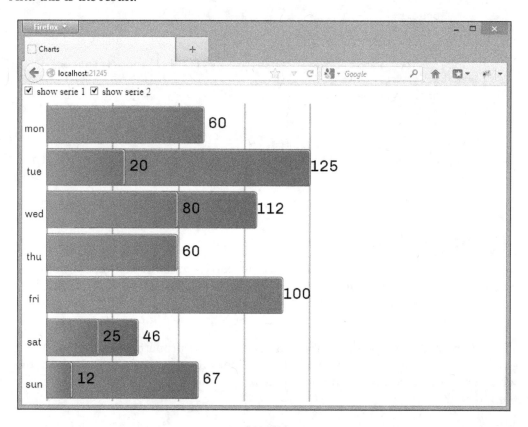

Of course, neither does this last implementation work, nor is it easily obtainable, in browsers where CSS `transform` properties are not supported.

Creating pie charts using only CSS and HTML

In conclusion of this chapter, I want to introduce to you a very smart technique I learned from Patrick Denny (Head Noggin of Atomic Noggin Enterprises) for creating pie charts out of nothing but HTML and CSS.

The core of the technique focuses on how to obtain a slice of the chart of the desired size; this is achieved using the `clip` and `border-radius` properties on an HTML structure like this (we can create a new `pie.html` file):

```
<div class="hold">
<div class="slice slice1"></div>
</div>
```

First of all, we create a circle using a `.slice` selector and the `border-radius` property; we cut the circle in half.

```
.slice{
  position: absolute;
  width: 200px;
  height: 200px;
  clip: rect(0px,100px,200px,0px);
  border-radius: 100px;
}
```

Then, we cut off the other half of the circle by using the `clip` property, as follows:

```
.hold {
  position: absolute;
  width: 200px;
  height: 200px;
  clip: rect(0px,200px,200px,100px);
}
```

Now, using the `clip` property on `.hold`, we cut off the other half of the circle with the `width` and `height` properties set to `200px`. The last step is easy, we can show a slice of the pie of a chosen size by rotating `.slice` by the correspondent angle:

```
.slice1{
  -moz-transform: rotate(30deg);
  -webkit-transform: rotate(30deg);
```

```
    -o-transform: rotate(30deg);
    transform: rotate(30deg);
    background-color: red;
}
```

And here's the result:

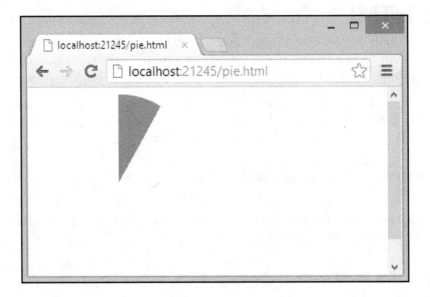

By stacking some of these HTML structures one on top of the other, a fully-functional and pure CSS pie chart can be obtained.

A more detailed procedure is described on Patrick's blog at `http://atomicnoggin.ca/blog/2010/02/20/pure-css3-pie-charts/`.

Summary

In this chapter, we've used resources and techniques introduced earlier in the book to build a rather complex visual graph. This project shows how CSS can be used to develop components that otherwise would require JavaScript or additional technologies such as Flash or Silverlight.

Index

append function 200
application.scss file 243
aria-required property 19
arrow
  creating 203, 204
  moving 204, 205
  trembling 208, 210
arrows
  creating 138
article element 48

B

background 13
background-color property 250, 251
background function 199
background-position 202
background property 183
background-size property
  about 14, 202
  contain property 14
  cover property 14
  length property 14
  percentage property 14
balloon styling 26, 27
bar chart
  creating 241-243
bar labels
  creating 246, 247
bars
  designing 247-249
Black star 43
blur function 187
border-box option 81
border-radius 173
border-radius property 172, 175, 250
box-flex property 93
box-orient property 94
box-shadow mask 52
box-shadow property 41, 49
box-sizing 81
bullets
  styling 128
buttons
  about 31
  active state 51
  checked state, adding 52

colors, adding 52
labels, adding 43, 44
mouse clicks 44, 45

C

camera
  moving 232-234
chart
  about 249-251
  rotating 257, 259
chart lines 251, 252
chart series
  about 253, 255
  animations, adding 256
checked state
  adding 52
clip property 259
closest-corner parameter 37
closest-side parameter 37
coin-operated push button 32
color property 69
colors
  adding 52, 74, 75
compass
  about 191
  and Internet Explorer 10 217, 218
  documentation, URL 193
  installing 192, 193
compass-animation 209
config.rb file 193
contain parameter 37
contain property 14
content-box option 81
content property 19, 24, 246
cos function 201
counter() function-like command 24
counter-increment property 22
counters
  implementing 25, 26
counter(variable name) declaration 24
cover parameter 37
cover property 14
CSS
  applying 125
  filters 187
  reset 194, 195

flexie
  adding 245
FlowingData
  URL 90
font-size property 195
footer element 26
form
  creating 10
  HTML code, writing 10

G

gallery
  randomness, adding 162, 163
gauge
  animating 206
  background size 200
  implementing, in Internet
    Explorer 8 213-215
  indicator 206, 208
  position 200
  structure 191, 192, 197, 198
  tick marks 198, 199
  value, displaying 210
gauge-background mixin 218
gauge-tick-marks function 217
Gecko
  parallax scrolling, implementing 158, 160
Generate button 54
Generate! button 103
Google Chart Tools
  URL 241
Google Chrome 38
Google service 9
Google Web Fonts 9, 10
graceful degradation 28, 29
gradient
  about 35
  closest-corner parameter 37
  closest-side parameter 37
  contain parameter 37
  cover parameter 37
  CSS3 gradients, syntax changes 40
  farthest-corner parameter 37
  farthest-side parameter 37
  linear-gradient 35

radial-gradient 35
  repeating-linear-gradient 35
  repeating-radial-gradient 35
  syntax 36
  types 35
gRaphael
  URL 241
grayscale filter 189, 190

H

hashchange event 119
height property 248
Highcharts
  URL 241
**hsl coordinate system (hue saturation
    lightness) 255**
HTML5
  attributes 11
HTML5 form validation model 18
html5shiv
  URL 10
HTML5 video element 171, 172
html element 156, 215
HTML menu
  animations 71
  colors, adding 74, 75
  creating 58
  first-level items, styling 61
  moving parts 66
  setup operations 58, 61
  sub menus, styling 64, 66
  transitions, adding 68, 69
HTML structure
  about 8, 9
  creating 222
http_path 193

I

icons
  within radio buttons, displaying 21, 23
IE10
  supporting 56
image gallery
  bullets, styling 128, 129
  CSS, applying 125-127

style attribute 127
stylesheet
  resetting 9, 10
sub menus
  styling 64, 65
SVG
  animations 182
  embedding 99
  embedding, ways 99
  targeting, with CSS 117

T

text
  masking with 185
text-shadow 41
this_bar_chart 243
top$100% property 247
transform: perspective property 159
transform-origin property 133, 160
transform property 120, 152, 206, 215, 257
transform-style property 133
transition: all 1s property 74
transition property 68, 206
transitions
  adding 68-70
translateZ property 113

V

value class 243
video element
  about 171
  masking, with text 185, 186

W

WAI-ARIA specification
  URL 19
WebKit
  parallax scrolling, implementing 156-158
WebKit-specific properties
  -webkit-mask-attachment
    (background-attachment) 183
  -webkit-mask (background) property 183
  -webkit-mask-box-image
    (border-image) 184
  -webkit-mask-clip (background-clip) 183
  -webkit-mask-composite
    (background-composite) 184
  -webkit-mask-image
    (background-image) 184
  -webkit-mask-origin
    (background-origin) 184
  -webkit-mask-position
    (background-position) 184
  -webkit-mask-repeat
    (background-repeat) 184

Y

yepnope.js
  URL 54

Z

z-index value 138
zooming user interface. *See* ZUI
ZUI 89

 Thank you for buying
Designing Next Generation Web Projects with CSS3

About Packt Publishing

Packt, pronounced 'packed', published its first book "*Mastering phpMyAdmin for Effective MySQL Management*" in April 2004 and subsequently continued to specialize in publishing highly focused books on specific technologies and solutions.

Our books and publications share the experiences of your fellow IT professionals in adapting and customizing today's systems, applications, and frameworks. Our solution based books give you the knowledge and power to customize the software and technologies you're using to get the job done. Packt books are more specific and less general than the IT books you have seen in the past. Our unique business model allows us to bring you more focused information, giving you more of what you need to know, and less of what you don't.

Packt is a modern, yet unique publishing company, which focuses on producing quality, cutting-edge books for communities of developers, administrators, and newbies alike. For more information, please visit our website: www.packtpub.com.

Writing for Packt

We welcome all inquiries from people who are interested in authoring. Book proposals should be sent to author@packtpub.com. If your book idea is still at an early stage and you would like to discuss it first before writing a formal book proposal, contact us; one of our commissioning editors will get in touch with you.

We're not just looking for published authors; if you have strong technical skills but no writing experience, our experienced editors can help you develop a writing career, or simply get some additional reward for your expertise.

PUBLISHING

Responsive Web Design
with HTML5 and CSS3

Learn responsive design using HTML5 and CSS3 to adapt
websites to any browser or screen size

Ben Frain

Responsive Web Design with HTML5 and CSS3

ISBN: 978-1-84969-318-9　　　　Paperback: 324 pages

Learn responsive design using HTML5 and CSS3 to adapt websites to any browser or screen size

1. Everything needed to code websites in HTML5 and CSS3 that are responsive to every device or screen size

2. Learn the main new features of HTML5 and use CSS3's stunning new capabilities including animations, transitions, and transformations

3. Real-world examples show how to progressively enhance a responsive design while providing fall backs for older browsers

HTML5 Games
Development by Example

Create six fun games using the latest HTML5, Canvas, CSS,
and JavaScript techniques

Beginner's Guide

Makzan

HTML5 Games Development by Example: Beginner's Guide

ISBN: 978-1-84969-126-0　　　　Paperback: 352 pages

Create six fun games using the latest HTML5, Canvas, CSS, and JavaScript techniques

1. Learn HTML5 game development by building six fun example projects

2. Full, clear explanations of all the essential techniques

3. Covers puzzle games, action games, multiplayer, and Box 2D physics

4. Use the Canvas with multiple layers and sprite sheets for rich graphical games

Please check **www.PacktPub.com** for information on our titles

Drupal 7 Module Development

ISBN: 978-1-84951-116-2   Paperback: 420 pages

Create your own Drupal 7 modules from scratch

1.   Specifically written for Drupal 7 development

2.   Write your own Drupal modules, themes, and libraries

3.   Discover the powerful new tools introduced in Drupal 7

4.   Learn the programming secrets of six experienced Drupal developers

Learning jQuery 1.3

ISBN: 978-1-84719-670-5   Paperback: 444 pages

Better Interaction Design and Web Development with Simple JavaScript Techniques

1.   An introduction to jQuery that requires minimal programming experience

2.   Detailed solutions to specific client-side problems

3.   For web designers to create interactive elements for their designs

4.   For developers to create the best user interface for their web applications

Please check **www.PacktPub.com** for information on our titles